"Joe White knows more about teenagers than anyone in North America."
—Dr. James Dobson, president of Focus on the Family

"Just like the man who wrote it, this book is a rare mixture of genuineness, gentleness, and drive. Like no one else out there, Joe White knows how to get to the real heart of parenting."
—Gary Smalley, president of Today's Family

"Joe White is a master at moving kids toward Christ."
—John Trent, president of Encouraging Words

"I've watched Joe speak to young people about Christ, I've seen how he drops everything just to get into the heart of a kid. Joe puts 150 percent into loving young adults—finding out who they are and where they're at in this crazy world of ours. I don't know anyone who has spent more time with kids than Joe. He knows what's going on in their lives. And I feel blessed to call him one of my best friends."
—Michael W. Smith, singer and songwriter

"This book is a tear-jerker, a heart-throbber, and a real motivator to me to love my kids. It has also helped equip me to do the job. The champs in my home will be the real winners from the many new tips I've picked up in this book. Thanks, Joe!"
—Josh McDowell, author of Why Wait? and More Than a Carpenter

"No parental responsibility is more important than passing on the torch of faith to our children, and Joe White is just the person to equip us for that task."
—John Nieder, president of The Art of Family Living

"Joe White is one of God's real men. He has a raging love affair with God and with kids from all over the world—and he wants to give each of them an opportunity to be their very best. I wish I could put this book in every home in America."
—Tim Hansel, author of What Kids Need Most in a Dad and You Gotta Keep Dancin'

"After a lifetime of experience with young people I have concluded that unconditional love provides their greatest source of inner security and feelings of satisfaction with life. This book will help a lot of parents realize how important it is to 'fall in love' with their youngsters all over again—and to keep at it."
—Art Linkletter, author of Kids Say the Darndest Things

What Kids Wish Parents Knew about Parenting

Please join us by the fire in the family room of our Ozark
Mountain home to share hot chocolate with melting
marshmallows floating on top . . . and
to break the bread of friendship together.
It is indeed a privilege to be with you.

What Kids Wish Parents Knew about Parenting

What You Need to Know Before It's Too Late

JOE WHITE

HOWARD
PUBLISHING CO.

Our purpose at Howard Publishing is to:

- *Increase faith* in the hearts of growing Christians
- *Inspire holiness* in the lives of believers
- *Instill hope* in the hearts of struggling people everywhere

Because He's coming again!

What Kids Wish Parents Knew about Parenting © 1998 by Joe White
All rights reserved. Printed in the United States of America

Published by Howard Publishing Co., Inc.,
3117 North 7th Street, West Monroe, Louisiana 71291-2227

03 04 05 06 07   10 9 8 7 6 5 4 3

Library of Congress Cataloging-in-Publication Data
White, Joe, 1948–
    What kids wish parents knew about parenting : what you need to
know before it's too late / Joe White.
        p. cm.
    ISBN 1-58229-341-4 (pbk.)
    1. Child rearing—Religious aspects—Christianity. 2. Parenting—Religious
aspects—Christianity. I. Title.
HQ769.3.W48 1998
649'.1—dc21   98-7097
                                                                  CIP

Interior design by Desktop Miracles, Inc., Dallas, Texas

Scripture quotations not otherwise marked are from the New American Standard Bible
© 1973 by The Lockman Foundation.

To Trevor

Like a giant oak,
memories of you will outlive us all.

As I commence writing a book that I frequently have prayed will affect every aspect of parenting for every mother and father who reads it, a familiar lump nags within my neck, making difficult a simple swallow.

The lump in my throat is a tumor I've grown to appreciate. Surgically, it is impossible to get to . . . for it's a lump of grief, accompanied often by watery eyes and an empty heart. I'm lonesome for a man who was my second daddy, who was killed in a plane crash several years ago.

To Dr. Trevor E. Mabery, my encourager, my "other" father, my example, and my friend . . . this book is dedicated.

As he successfully loved two boys and a girl of his own into their young adult lives, Trevor's model as a daddy was unsurpassed. His unconditional love was poured out on his most fortunate family.

He was also a model of success in his profession. So skilled was he that even the famous Dr. Mayo let him perform his most difficult operations when Trevor was still a young surgeon in the formative years of his career. Small children born with severely deformed faces left Dr. Mabery's operating room with beautiful new eyes, mouths, and noses . . . thanks to this man and his skillful team.

Internationally known and in great demand, Trevor never missed a football game when a son was on the field. For years, he and his son rolled newspapers together at 5:30 A.M. for the boy's paper route. During hunting season, he and his sons were together in the duck blind or deer stand, weekend after weekend.

His smile never dimmed. He lived always for his God and his family—until the fateful moment when the twin-engine plane he was aboard couldn't climb out of a beautiful Rocky Mountain valley, and crashed into Dead Indian Peak some fifteen thousand feet above sea level.

His reputation as a dad lives on . . . still influencing my life . . . and permeating the pages of this book.

I want to offer deep expressions of gratitude to my dear mom, for always making our house a home; to Gary Smalley and Josh McDowell, for their loving hearts and wisdom in helping me develop this book; and to Johnny Koons, for running the show while I took time off to write.

CONTENTS

PART IV

Safe at Home

PART V

Tomorrow's Family Album

FOREWORD

Today, more than ever before, there is a movement of men and women seeking to love their children. Fathers are spending more quality and quantity time with their children. Mothers are realizing that their children are more important than their goals for career and achievement. But this movement is threatened by a roadblock that could bring its momentum to a complete stop. That roadblock is the lack of practical methods and skills on how to love our children.

As a father of thirty-one years, I have tremendous empathy for all the fathers and mothers who want to love their children but don't know how. *What Kids Wish Parents Knew about Parenting* provides a wonderful blueprint for how to love your children. Joe White brings more than thirty years of hands-on experience with hundreds of thousands of kids. Not only do Joe and his wife, Debbie-Jo, have four of their own children, Joe leads the nation's largest Christian sports camp, Kanakuk Kamps. Every summer more than fifteen thousand kids, ages eight to eighteen, spend time in a Christ-centered program that changes lives. I know how effective Kanakuk Kamp is because all three of my children were campers and counselors over a ten-year period. I have seen first-hand how Joe White's programs communicate personal love and growth to thousands of kids and especially to my own.

Because Joe has spent thousands of hours listening to kids share their needs, he knows what kids wish their parents knew about parenting. Many children want their parents' time, many want their laughter, many need their ears, and many want their hearts. Joe White also shares his own failures and his struggles to find the balance between a busy lifestyle and making his own family his first priority.

If you'll take the time to read this book and apply its principles, you will see a transformation in your children. I challenge you to invest the courage and energy to love your children. Joe White will show you how!

—GARY SMALLEY
PRESIDENT, TODAY'S FAMILY

*All theories aside . . . meet America's youth and the homes
that make them the kind of young people they are.*

PART I

The Lights Are On,
But . . .

The chains of habit are too weak to be felt until

they're (almost) too strong to be broken.

orphan \or-fan\ n. 1. A child whose parents have left him physically. 2. A child whose parents have left him emotionally. 3. Can be evidenced by a half-smoked joint in a jeans pocket or a sexy love note left inadvertently in a drawer or a citation from the local police.

1

Slipping Away

We're so busy giving our kids what we didn't have
that we don't take time to give them what we did have.

I hate to sound selfish, like everything's mine,
but please don't get mad when I ask for your time.

I'll never forget the day I hit bottom in my career as a daddy.

I first started realizing my failure the day my oldest son's babysitter taught him how to ride his bike. It's such a monumental achievement for a boy—in fact, five decades haven't erased the memory of reaching that milestone in my own life. But Brady had to experience it without me.

Busy (as usual) with work, I met Brady for a quick lunch that day, and he beamed with excitement as he shared the news.

I had all the right things to say: "Wow, Brady! That's great! I'm so proud of you." Then I added, "Brady, can I come watch you ride your bike later this afternoon?"

The response from my sweet, gentle-spirited six-year-old fell on me like an avalanche. "No, Dad, that's okay. You're busy in the summer."

I'm fighting the tears again as I remember the deep remorse I felt. He had opened my heart more skillfully than a surgeon.

I was losing my son.

He knew it, and I knew it.

In my job as president of a large summer camp complex, I was so busy rescuing other people's kids that my own were drowning. And the problem—as I knew Brady couldn't help but discover as time went on—was that I'm busy not only in the summer but also in the fall, winter, and spring.

Brady . . . he was so little then, but he had the super imagination and the super-sensitivity that made his daddy work harder on smoothing his many rough edges and his hard-driving disposition. With a quick look into the future, I could see Brady as a teenager in someone else's counseling office trying to sort out his bitterness toward a father too busy to show he cared.

Not long afterward, my youngest daughter was attending one of our short-term camps. We agreed to abide by the rule requesting parents not to visit their children for the entire week. (That's tough!)

On the fifth night, Courtney got a touch of homesickness. She began to cry, and her counselor came to her bed to give her some hugs and tenderness.

"Corky, don't cry anymore. You'll be home in two days, and you'll get to see your daddy and everything."

"I never get to see my daddy!" was her bold protest.

When the week was over, the camp director came to my house. "Sit down," he said abruptly. I sat down, wondering what this was all about.

He told me about the conversation between the counselor and Courtney—little Corky, with long, blond hair and dimples that can't help but melt her daddy's heart. Even when the lower lip was out in an occasional protest, a few tickles and funny faces could bring the dimples back to their rightful place.

"What are you going to do about it?" he asked.

I squirmed. He looked deep into my eyes.

The phone rang. As I went to answer it, the intercom buzzed. Then someone came to the door with an emergency. After responding to all three, I sat back down. He was still looking intently at me.

"I asked you, 'What are you going to do about it?' "

"I don't know . . . it's hard . . . there are so many demands."

"Joe, who are the most important people in your life?"

"My family."

"You're not showing it!"

He sat there and didn't give an inch. Finally, I agreed to some commitments.

This book is an expression of my gratitude for my months of open-heart surgery that summer. To this day, I'm carrying out the commitments I made back then. It's still hard. The demands are still there. In fact, they're getting worse. But my priorities changed. I aborted almost everything from my life that stood between my children and me. The use-of-time knife stripped away most of the fat that surrounded the lean meat of necessity.

My wife and I continued the struggle to accomplish more during the necessary hours of daily labor, and in the remaining hours to prioritize time with our children above anything else during these years while they were still at home. We were wonderfully amazed that there was even enough time for a few luxuries.

Brady became my best male friend. I worked early and late when he wasn't available, so that when he came home, I could grab a bat and ball or a go-cart or a fishing rod or a made-up adventure, all for the honor of getting to be by his side for a few golden ticks of the clock. His brother Cooper and his sisters Jamie and Courtney . . . all of them became World's Best Companions to me.

The four young children who captured my heart are now young adults. The lessons I learned and put into practice then continue to reap a joyous harvest.

Allow me, in love, to ask you the same question the camp director asked me those many years ago: Who are the most important people in your life?

If it's your family . . . are you showing it?

If not . . . what are you going to do about it?

Just as during the early days of work on Mount Rushmore, when the explosives engineer was told to blast away all the granite that didn't look like the face of a president, so I urge you to strip away—with dyna-mite, if necessary—everything in your life that doesn't look like family gold.

champion \champ-e-un\ n. 1. A person who is willing to put other's needs before his own. 2. Every child who has parents willing to unleash his or her potential.

2

The Champs

All children are champs—with potential they're packed;
discovery alone is the element lacked.

Son, you're the greatest!
—HERMAN "SLEEPY" MORGAN

On that Father's Day morning, something told me I was being set up.

All four of my children bubbled with excitement as they led me to their playroom. I felt special to have all that attention from the ones I love the most.

Their eyes sparkled mischievously as they showed me a big white box on the playroom floor, wrapped in fourth-grader uniqueness with hand-drawn decorations on all six sides. It was so *big!*

"Hurry, Dad, open it up!" four little voices screamed in unison, as if from fear the box would pull a self-destruction act before I got to the contents.

As I bent down to pull off the customized wrapping paper, the box began to move, and I heard a whimpering, whining sound from inside.

Instantly I knew: I'd been framed!

"There's a puppy inside that thing!" I exclaimed. Soon the lid was attacked by eight tiny hands, and up popped an exuberant ball of black fur.

"Daddy, Daddy, can we keep it?"

"Happy Father's Day, Daddy!"

"Don't you just love him?"

"Let's name him Champ!"

The sounds of excitement filled the house.

I'd been set up to the max. Even their mother was in on the deal. How does a daddy turn down a Father's Day gift—hand wrapped in crayon-colored paper, no less?

"Okay, gang," I accepted cautiously, "but only if you take care of him."

"Sure, Daddy, we'll be happy to!"

Champ was sired by my big black four-year-old retriever, Pro. Pro, who was from the bloodline of Old Yeller, Hollywood's most famous Labrador retriever, now had a major problem: He had to share everything with that yipping, biting, pestering Champ, who was nothing but an annoyance—to both of us.

Champ may have been my new Lab . . . but in my heart, I didn't really claim him.

Our nation's homes are full of little "Champs." Some are boys, some girls. Some are toddlers, and some are teens. They legally belong to a mom and/or a dad, but they've never felt totally claimed.

In various ways they send up their signals from every city, crying out for unconditional love and acceptance from their too-busy parents.

Almost every day I get letters from teenagers across America who feel like little Champ. One recent letter—from Amy, age seventeen—epitomizes their cry:

> I've always wanted so badly to please my father and my mother. I hated to be yelled at. Every time I was caught doing something wrong, I felt worthless at home and at school. It was very embarrassing for me to get into trouble. My mom, who I've always been close to, kicked me out of the house and started packing my things just to get back at my dad. I kept

thinking to myself, "Is she serious? Where should I go? I have nowhere to go." The scars run pretty deep.

After Pro and I had tolerated Champ for a couple of summer months, an interesting event forever altered Champ's stature in my heart. The two dogs were bounding through our summer camp, with Champ playing his usual game of jump-up-and-bite-Pro's-neck, lips, and-ears. As always, Pro used every ounce of self-control in his pedigree to keep from making supper out of his menacing offspring.

The two black beauties apparently stopped at our huge outdoor swimming pool—which was closed for the day—to get a drink, and Pro fell in. Labradors are born swimmers, but the distance between the water's surface and the deck around it was about four inches higher than a dog can reach. After what must have been fifteen to thirty minutes, a teenage boy walking by the pool saw what happened next: As Pro began to go under, little sixteen-pound Champ leaned down, bit Pro in the lip, and with some internal shot of adrenaline pulled his sixty-five-pound daddy out of the water.

Champ found a new place in our home that night. Same pup, same yip, same disposition, but he had a new status. Now he was a hero, and we treated him as he had deserved to be treated all along. He was stroked, praised, caressed, and honored.

Champ now owned a special place in my heart—a place valued all the more when, two months later, Pro was struck and killed while crossing a highway. Now I regard that whimpering, oversized box as the best Father's Day present in all the wonderful years since I first received my most cherished title, "Daddy."

Do you have a Champ in your home?

After working, counseling, living, and talking with hundreds of thousands of teenagers during the past twenty-five years, I've found that there's a Champ in every one—if that child's parents will only take the time to discover the vein of gold in their child's heart.

All successful homes have this in common: the discovery of champions.

It can be done in all kinds of homes—two-parent homes, single-parent homes, or homes where grandparents assume the role of Mom and Dad. My grandmother found a champion in my mom while raising her all alone. What a job she did.

My wife is truly a champion, though her father (a Navy test pilot) was killed when she was four years old. She, too, had a mom who courageously and patiently raised her and her two brothers until a stepdad came into the picture.

My daddy was fortunate to have both parents there at home to do the job and even more fortunate that both of them recognized his great potential and allowed it to bloom.

The discovery of champions can happen in your family too.

When Champ was two years old a sudden, tragic death took him seemingly long before his time was due. My only consolation was that before it was too late, we learned to treat him like the champion he was.

Our kids' lives, too, are so fragile, and the short time we're allowed to be with them races by . . . there never seems to be enough.

Whatever age your children are . . . today is a great day to bring out the best in each of their lives.

Two Mothers Who Wouldn't Give Up

Chris's Mom

I said it would never happen to my son.

Until his seventh-grade year, Chris was polite, loving, and content. When I saw the plastic bag of dried-up leaves in his pocket, I didn't even know what it was.

The marijuana habit led to LSD, cocaine, and hash. He lied about it habitually, and I so wanted to believe him—love hopes all things. He made up wild and crazy stories that I wanted to be true. But I couldn't deny the hard facts that followed his footsteps.

His grades went down. He became a skilled player of video games to win drug money, but it wasn't enough. He stole from our home and burglarized others.

He sold drugs to his friends. While in the ninth grade, he was suspended from school for dealing drugs in the library. I was humiliated. I was scared. I wanted him to know I still loved him.

I'm told a common first mistake made by parents who learn their child is using drugs is to look the other way and pretend it isn't happening. A second is to look for a quick, easy remedy. A third, when you've tried everything humanly possible and all has failed, is to give up.

We went through stages of all three. But every night we got on our knees in prayer. We'd made mistakes as Chris's parents—no doubt about it. But through it all, we loved him while hating his sin.

Chris never ran away . . . but I did. The pressure got to me. I checked into a hotel for two nights to struggle with God.

While there, I began to see that drugs weren't the enemy. They were just weapons. It was a spiritual battle we were in. The enemy was after my son, my family, my marriage.

I faced all the *what ifs*. I was sure Chris would either commit suicide, die of an overdose, or be killed in a car accident. It was happening in front of my eyes, and I was powerless. I had tried everything but couldn't rescue him from his problems.

I decided I would trust God, no matter what. That was the first and best step. I found His peace in that hotel room.

When I went home things were the same, but I was different.

Chris had become a pro at deceit, a con artist. He hated himself, but on his own he couldn't change. I knew something drastic had to be done. A month at a Christian summer camp helped, but it wasn't enough time. A year at a special home for troubled youth also helped, but even there he smuggled in drugs and had the wrong friends.

Then two men who were constructing a Christian camp took Chris in and gave him five months of solitary confinement, hard labor, and love. He would work all day, listen to Christian music and go through Bible studies in the evening, and drop exhausted into bed at 8:00 P.M. The work kept his mind off drugs and built his self-esteem, something he drastically needed. Phoning him from home, we continued to pour on the encouragement while making it clear we couldn't allow his former behavior.

Then he came home. He was now seventeen years old. In another year he would be out on his own. We wanted to believe he was well. But he returned to his old friends, too weak to fight their influence.

Then I heard about Tom Johnson, a wonderful cowboy with a youth ranch in Arkansas. We sent Chris there, and on the way he gave up fighting. Miraculously, all the Christ-centered experience he'd been given, plus our continuing love and unceasing prayers, finally took root in his heart. He asked Jesus Christ to take over his life.

At the ranch he saw an inspirational Christian model in Tom. On the first morning there, at daybreak, Chris helped Tom deliver a calf. As the sun came up, Chris felt as if God were showing him a new life. He didn't tell anyone at the time, because he felt he had talked too much. Now he wanted to show.

He hasn't done a drug since that sunrise.

The next time we saw him, he gave his dad a great big hug.

Chris will soon graduate from college.

He shares Christ with druggies and punk rockers. With his skateboard and drums, he gets into places a preacher could never go.

He'll always be on the cutting edge.

Sharon's Mom

We were some of the "beautiful people" in our community—Robert worked night and day while I played tennis at the country club—and our teenage daughter, Sharon, was an ornament. I had to take time away from my tennis to drive her to school. (Kids deserve better.)

I subtly gave Sharon pressure to stay on top. She just did what I asked her to. When I woke up she was a sizzling sixteen-year-old brunette with big blue eyes and a body filled with alcohol and drugs.

In three hundred and sixty-five days she spiraled down from a "most likely to succeed" to a drunk and a druggie.

No one felt worse about it than she did. She couldn't stop because her group of friends expected her to live up to her new image. Kids are so totally driven by acceptance. She didn't feel acceptance at home, so she got it from whomever she could.

We were so far off as parents. We let the TV set—instead of our example—be our child's value education. If you don't want your kids to drink, don't drink. What you say doesn't matter. Kids learn (or miss learning) responsibility at home.

Things had gotten out of control in such a short time. Robert got scared that we were losing each other over Sharon. "You're giving her too much of your mind," he pleaded with me. "I'm giving her up. We won't fight over her. She's yours now—yours to love, yours to discipline."

I prayed desperately. *Please take her back, Robert.*

Sharon ran.

I felt like someone had blasted me with a shotgun, and I was full of holes, bleeding.

We got her back. Then I tried everything. I played rough at first. I took away all privileges—the phone, the TV set, everything. But the love wasn't there to back up the ultrastrict discipline.

Next I tried to identify with her. I took her places. I drank with her. I wanted her to see how to drink "responsibly." I was desperate and ready to do anything.

My heart was repeatedly broken during those times. She lied and misled us. She said it was better, but it wasn't. I felt so foolish. She said she hated us, but she was really saying, "Help!" She felt so abused and so guilty.

Today she says, "Thanks for not giving up on me after I gave up on myself."

Here's how the turnaround happened.

Robert and I submitted our whole family to some solid biblical counselors. They told us to keep on believing in Sharon. At first we reacted to that: "Believe in what?" But eventually we completely adopted our child in our hearts . . . with all of her problems.

Next, we inventoried our own lives and began to fill our home with consistency. We gave ourselves more lovingly to each other and to our younger children.

I love wine, but when I caught my second daughter and her friends downing some whiskey (from our overstocked liquor cabinet) on their way out of the house to a party, I knew our social drinking had to go too. (Why do we play our kids for such fools sometimes?)

We continued over the next six years to rebuild our ties with Sharon. As we forged the new relationship, we wondered: How do you go back and undo all the crossed-up circuits? She had been programmed all wrong.

We didn't quit. We lived on our knees, it seemed.

Sharon protested, "You've never been a mother to me, and I can't accept it now." But she did need an authority. I kept my mouth shut and listened to her. Then I listened some more. When she finished expressing her thoughts, I'd ask, "What are you thinking? . . . What are you feeling? . . . How can I help you?" I filled her with honest praise. Then

I'd state my position. Sometimes she'd get so angry.

Robert and I worked at being more honest. We became more available to our kids. In everything, we strove to be authentic.

With the help of the Christian youth and family counselors, we began to see daylight. In a couple of years, the storm was over, and our skies became only partly cloudy.

Today we are close. Our house is a home. It still rains here sometimes, but there are also sunny days to enjoy.

I believe the tragic years with Sharon actually saved us from a lifetime of casual misery. It was worth the trouble to begin to understand each other and really get to know the power of Jesus Christ in a family.

Today as he left for college, my nineteen-year-old son said, "Mom, wouldn't you rather be called a great mom than a great tennis player or a corporate officer?" Then he added, "You're a great mom!"

Maybe he's exaggerating with the "great." I think "great-ful" (grateful!) is a better word for me.

apathy \a-puh-the\ n. 1. What parents feel about today's rapidly deterioriating society. 2. What children feel when their parents won't look at them.

3

Who Cares?

Think I'll buy a forty-four
Give 'em all a surprise
Think I'm gonna kill myself
Cause a little suicide.
—ELTON JOHN

Several years alo, Elvis Presley's colorful stepbrother spent some time with us at our summer sports camp. Elvis loved music, but Rick Stanley loved kids.

As we talked about the plight of the modern teenager, Rick told me of another brother's backstage encounter with David Lee Roth, the former lead singer of Van Halen, who sang of suicide, drugs, torture, sex, rebellion, and perversion. After a lengthy conversation about Elvis, his fame, his music, and his tragic death, the brother asked Roth the same question I would want to ask him: "David, what do you think about the thousands of kids out there in the crowd tonight who are getting stoned, wasted, messed up?"

With a blunt, cold stare, Roth answered, "Who cares?"

At least he was honest. Roth didn't seem to care about anyone but himself. But the problem was that so many vulnerable kids looked up to him. At a typical concert, twenty thousand of them—averaging fourteen years of age—would pay a half million dollars and practically break down the doors to partake in two hours of visual and verbal pornography. The next day at school they'd wear their new rock T-shirts to celebrate their evening with a hero.

Who are your kids' heroes?

They're displayed on the posters on the walls of their rooms. Look into their eyes. What do you see?

My breakfast guest one morning was a seventeen-year-old boy who was six-foot-two and weighed a hundred and ninety pounds. He was as lost as a baby billy goat. He came from a wonderful home, but nine months with the wrong three friends—and who knows how many dozen marijuana cigarettes—had sent him into a tailspin and turned his home upside down. To my amazement, this confused teenager told me over breakfast how both he and his best friend were introduced to pot by the friend's father—right in their home.

Does that make you fighting mad?

What about the homes that expose their children to 18,000 murders, 75,000 scenes of physical intimacy between unmarried partners, 75,000 commercials whose basic message is: "Take a pill for a problem," and 66,000 commercials that say: "Drink alcohol for fun"? Those are the actual estimates of what a kid sees on television while growing up in the average America home.

The subtlety of this invasion is crafty, and the hypocrisy behind it is incredible. It's an intruder that slips into our homes like a cunning burglar, and parents indifferent to it are cultivating disaster for their kids.

Children become what they think about—it's a principle as certain as gravity. So what type of influence at home is worse—the father who brings home marijuana or the "average" amount of television viewing?

Every album your kids play, every concert they attend, every television show they watch . . . each one is like a stepdad temporarily taking over your role of teacher, coach, and friend. Is this the kind of stand-in you want for yourself?

Parents are the decision makers. The federal government won't help our kids avoid the worst influences. The city council won't. Our neighbors won't.

The responsibility is yours and mine.

So who cares?

You do.

I do.

How much are we showing it?

PART II

A Homeowner's Guide to the Family Gold Mine

This is how you can tell a father:

He's a man who will play with you even though he

has friends his own age to play with.

—FROM A FATHER'S DAY CARD

(© HALLMARK CARDS, INC.)

light \lit\ n. 1. As different from dark as a home is from a house. 2. The energy given off by family members enjoying each other; the radiance of Mom and Dad's love and approval; the aura of smiling and laughing together.

4

The Light That's Nearest

You may beat us on the road, but we'll get you at home.
—Sparky Anderson

Today I can hear a cry—a desperate scream—from the kids growing up in our nation. They're crying for help!

The phone rings often in my home. Parents call with desperate questions . . . searching for an answer, a place, a person to turn to for help with a "lost" teenager. As I write now I've just hung up from talking with a frustrated stepmother of a seventeen-year-old boy. She and the boy's father have tried psychiatrists, family therapists, drugs, and several in-home techniques prescribed for handling rebellious children.

I know the boy wasn't "born to be wild." But as I talked with her, she told me how in his earlier years the boy had been shipped from one home to the other during the breakup of his parents' marriage. I wondered what would have happened if he had gotten more of his parents' love and attention back then.

"We've done everything," the stepmother said to me. "There's no hope."

What a tragedy! To realize "there's nothing else we can do" must be the toughest admission in any parent's life. But having known many people in this situation, I want to say, "*Yes*, there is something more you can do!" Even in the desperate stage, I've seen parents still willing to do anything, give anything, sacrifice anything to save their prized possession, their teenage child . . . and many are finding success.

Look Out, Mr. Gallup!

USA Today, Seventeen magazine, *Source* magazine, and *Reader's Digest* have published such statistical estimates as these:

- Of teenagers who drink, one in ten will become an alcoholic. Three to five of the remaining nine will have serious drinking problems. There are three to five million teen alcoholics growing up in America today.
- Of all the fourteen-year-old girls alive today, 40 percent will become pregnant by their nineteenth birthday.
- Sixty percent of all church-involved teenagers are sexually active.
- Eighty-four percent of all teenage boys believe that premarital sex is acceptable.
- Every year, 500,000 teenage girls in America have abortions.
- Every seventy-eight seconds, a teenager attempts suicide in America.
- Sixty-seven percent of America's ninth graders say they lied to their parents some time during the past twelve months.

These crazy numbers depress parents and make newlywed couples want to give up on having kids before they even get started.

But look out, Mr. Gallup! I've been doing a little research on my own, and I'd like to share with you encouraging evidence that kids are able, ready, and willing to go against their generation's trends—if parents do their part.

I spend each summer at our camps with five thousand kids from forty or so states. They range in age from eight to eighteen. With a staff-to-kid ratio of 1 to 3.5, my staff members and I get to know these kids well.

After surveying a thousand of them, I found that kids are still moldable lumps of clay. And they will receive whatever handprints give them the most attention. No matter what new theory secular humanists would like to sell us, I believe children have an innate, genetically programmed desire to be primarily molded by their mom and dad.

More than 80 percent of our camp's teenagers say they are against premarital sex. Ninety-two percent are against illegal drugs. The majority don't drink alcohol.

Why are these kids so different from their peers? Here's the kicker . . .

- Ninety-five percent of the boys indicate that their fathers regularly tell them "I love you." Seventy-nine percent of the fathers say it more than once a week, and 62 percent let those three magic words ring out every day.
- Ninety-eight percent of the girls say their mothers tell them regularly "I'm proud of you" or "You're doing a great job."
- Nine-one percent of the kids say their parents play games with them.
- Ninety-four percent say their fathers attend their athletic events.
- Ninety-seven percent of the boys say they get hugs from their dads.
- One hundred percent of the girls say they get hugs from their moms or dads.
- Recalling their childhoods, 100 percent of the girls remember having stories read to them by their mothers. Eighty-five percent of the boys recall having stories read to them by their dads.
- Eighty-nine percent of the boys say their fathers have taken them fishing.
- One hundred percent of the girls say their parents have taken them to Sunday school.
- Sixty-two percent of camp kids never drink.
- Eighty-seven percent of camp kids are virgins.
- Eighty-five percent of camp kids believe sex is okay only in marriage.

I once asked a friend, who was both an assistant coach of a professional football team and a successful businessman, what his goal in life was.

"Number one," he said, "is this: When my kids grow up, I want them to lead respectable, Christ-centered lives."

To that end he had made countless sacrifices in job opportunities and business ventures—some costing thousands of dollars—to keep his children in the same home, the same school, and the same church from year to year while they were growing up. For all his professional success, he hadn't lost sight of the importance of his family.

He never thought of himself as a superhero—but that's what he is to his kids. They respect him not because he makes a lot of money or because he works with a football team or because he can "speak their language." They esteem him because in their family he's a true leader, because he gives them the one thing he can't buy for them—himself.

In pursuing his goal, this man has faced far tougher opposition—seductive mass media, humanistic public education, depraved music, the drug culture, materialism, and more—than was ever encountered by the football teams he's coached. But it wasn't hard for me, sitting across from him as we talked in his office, to make a long mental list of the characteristics that mark him as a Christlike man. His starting lineup included love, enthusiasm, consistency, creativity, servanthood, discipline, and prayer.

These are the powerful weapons that make any mom or dad effective in defeating the villains of secular culture that attack our families and nation today.

You may not think of yourself as a superhero any more than this man did. In fact you may feel your family life is in serious trouble, that your kids feel more like orphans at home than like the children of a hero. But there's hope. There are actually encouraging signs in the heat of the battle. When given an adult friend who will really love them (faults and all) and who will give them a consistent example of good behavior to follow, most teenagers really want to do the right thing.

As I'm around so many thousands of teenagers and their families, I'm also excited about two other facts that are still true in spite of all the problems kids face today.

First, there are so many parents who do a truly great job with their kids. They are accepting the problems as challenges and meeting the challenges head-on with determination, self-sacrifice, and enthusiasm. They're being the heroes their kids need. The result is a number of kids who are more outstanding than any other generation of kids in history.

Second, the incredibly dangerous environment so many kids live in is actually bringing out the best in many of them. They're like saplings in a dense, high forest that grow straight and tall as they compete for light. The tougher the challenge, the more many kids stand committed to the right principles they've been taught and shown. I am truly amazed at the number of teenagers today who take a mature, positive stand for Christian values and moral living.

Close and Constant

One clear and beautiful Ozark evening last summer, I was walking my youngest daughter home after an evening youth rally. A splendid display of stars spangled overhead, a gift to enjoy from our Creator.

As Courtney and I marveled at the heavenlies, perhaps ten thousand feet above us I saw a jet airplane cruising through the night, its lights dimly visible as it prepared to land at an airport fifty miles away.

"Courtney, see those lights?" I asked as I pointed overhead.

She leaned back farther. "Yes, Daddy. What is it?"

"It's a jet, sweetheart. See how dim those lights are?"

"You can barely see them!"

Capturing a teaching moment, I continued, "Those lights are very, very bright when the plane is on the ground, but the further you're away from them, the dimmer they get. See that brightest star right near the plane? That star is thousands of times brighter than our sun, but it is more than ten million light years away, so it looks like a tiny dot in the sky."

"Wow, Dad, that's awesome!"

Just then a lightning bug only a few feet from us lit up brightly, almost like the startling flash of a camera. Just imagine—a lightning bug, whose tail measures only an eighth of an inch across, outshining an airplane's light that can illuminate a runway or a star that could make the sun look like a flickering candle in comparison.

The principle I observed began to grip me with excitement as I related it to parenting.

It's true that our kids are exposed to negative peer pressure at school, antifamily music at their friends' houses, seductive messages in television commercials—a whole assortment of modern-day bad influences. Their world is full of it, all presented in the brightest possible trappings to light up the eyes of children of all ages. It all looks so appealing! But I can shine my light before them . . . I can get my little flickering flame as close as possible to their eyes and keep that baby turned on every waking hour.

Our lights as Christian parents—the steady beam of our biblical, old-fashioned, pro-family values—may be small, and we can never give it the same seductive dazzle that the media fantasy-makers give their messages. But we can always keep our light just a whisper away from those precious pairs of eyes that look to us for leadership and direction.

Your Best Recruit

Men and women in every career tend to give their best to their professions, and often—all too often—spare only leftovers for the family. Their children realize what they're getting—and when peers come along and make them feel special by offering a beer or a joint or an enticing line of sexual allurement . . . guess where their allegiance goes?

Not long ago a successful collegiate coach called me into his office to join his wife and sixteen-year-old son for a "code three" emergency meeting about the family's quickly decaying relationships.

The coach was a busy man who gave seven-day work weeks to recruiting and training his world-class athletes. His wife was a divisional director for her company, responsible for training and supervising eighteen people.

The teenager was struggling. He wanted to obey his parents—who had set commendable guidelines for his social behavior—but when he came home on time, all too often no one was there to meet him. He felt he received no reinforcement from home as he faced alone the peer pressure from his social circles.

What could be done?

I encouraged the boy to continue honoring and obeying his parents. His puppy-dog eyes willingly gave away his deepest desire to comply. But there was also a strain in his countenance. He turned to his parents and pleaded with them to give him the strength, the courage—the relationship—to fight the lonely battle that any good kid must face in these difficult days for adolescents.

I thought of the great relationships the father had with his players and all the time and trouble he put into luring those blue-chip athletes to his West Coast campus. Dinners out, expensive lodging, impressive parties, numerous personal visits and phone calls were all part of the process. He was so successful. His players loved him.

Why couldn't he recruit his own son?

The father was open to instruction. We compared the value to his life of his son versus his players. He quickly agreed that on a scale of one to ten, his son was a ten and his athletes an eight or nine. Yet his son was being treated like a six, while the athletes received steady ten-and-a-half treatment.

We talked further at a later date. Eventually he left his coaching position to "recruit" his family. He sees now that he had taken for granted the son he loves so greatly. The boy, meanwhile, has turned away from some sources of negative peer influence.

Leaving that lucrative coaching position wasn't easy for the father. Choosing family over fame or fortune rarely is.

mind \mind\ n. 1. The only part of your child's body that keeps growing his whole life. 2. A way of thinking and feeling—determined by what its host sees and hears.

5

Close the Zoo

As [a man] thinks, so he is.
—PROVERBS 23:7

A man is what he thinks about all day long.
—RALPH WALDO EMERSON

*It's not how many fish you caught with your son; it's how
much you laughed when your tent started leaking.*

The animals in the Hong Kong Zoo were growing noticeably
fatigued, unhealthy, and more edgy and testy with each other as
the zoo grew in popularity and became more heavily visited by human
observers. So, according to the account in *Newsweek*, the zoo's directors
decided to give the animals some time off by closing the gates to the
public one day a week. The animals showed improvement, but still there
was more fighting and sickness than what seemed normal. Again the
directors met, and they decided to do what had never been done: Close
the zoo two days every week. The results were dramatic. Health and
playfulness were restored. The animals quit fighting. The directors were
amazed.

There's a lesson there for parents. If your kids aren't acting like the
maturing, lovable creatures they were meant to be . . . try closing the zoo.

If a crowd throwing peanuts can destabilize wild and noble beasts, think what's happening to young people targeted by the arrows of pornography, violence, degradation and other dangers launched continuously from today's music and media.

I have to say I'm the lucky one. Besides getting to be around my best teachers—the four kids who spent their growing-up years calling me Daddy—I have the privilege of raising kids for a living. Besides being around the thousands who come to our camps every summer, I travel frequently during the other seasons to youth rallies, school assemblies, and other events involving youth. And two blocks from our house live twenty searching teenagers in a resident care home.

Taken together, these encounters afford me the opportunity to speak with many thousands of teenagers each year. The best moments for learning come when, from out of the crowds, the hurting few approach one by one, seeking emotional help with "code three" urgency.

One weekend, for example, I spoke for ninety minutes to a group of several hundred teenagers at a leadership youth rally. Then I spent two and a half hours listening to a seventeen-year-old girl who has already had three abortions and is probably headed for more.

Such comprehensive exposure to kids has built up in me a mental computer bank with countless bits of information . . . problems and solutions . . . things that work and things that fail . . . knowledge of tears and laughter, of guilt and forgiveness, of frustrations and relief. It's all there. From it have come sound, deep, trustworthy patterns of counsel and teaching.

It all adds up to one overarching observation: Children become what they think about. And they think about what they see and hear.

Kids are the way they are because of what they're exposed to, what they fill their minds with.

The human brain was created to be programmed through the senses. The human body was developed to respond to the information stored in the mind. If a child sees and hears often enough about the pleasure of sexual sin, then that is exactly what you can expect that child to do as soon as he or she is able. One plus one always equals two.

The family's social and economic background doesn't matter. Our family enjoyed friendships with families in poor, inner-city situations as well as those among the nation's most financially secure—plus every range between. The background doesn't make a difference. What does make a difference is the number of hours the zoo is left open.

The Screen Scene

Browsing through the weekly *TV Guide* exposed quickly the underlying script that permeates the networks:

"When it comes to love, everything is relative" (the caption below a photo of a thirteen-year-old boy and girl embracing).

"A cabbie's search for his sister takes him into the dirtiest shadows of L.A.'s sex clubs."

"If there is a God . . . there must also be a devil. Tonight, terror is a religious experience."

"Smart, sexy, fearless—200 years ago in this room a beauty was driven to a crime of passion. Tonight it's about to happen again."

"Prom queen. Playboy centerfold. Movie star. Murder victim."

Sex. Passion. Seduction. Violence. Murder. This year, the average teen will spend just over twice as much time watching this immoral programming as she or he does in the classroom.

It all adds up.

Children become what they think about.

They think about what they see and hear.

We would never invite a murderer, a rapist, or a sexual pervert into our homes. But it is amazing how many of them we let in every day through television—on programs that make it all look so attractive to the growing, questioning minds of our children. It's pretty hard to expect children to practice personal morality, use clean language, and stiff-arm any enticement to drug abuse when a thirty-two-inch screen constantly promotes the opposite behaviors.

Music Makers, Life Takers

Resounding from the radio stations kids listen to most are lyrics like the following, which take advantage of music's power to stick like glue to young minds:

"Slide down to my knees, taste my sword" (Motley Crew, in the hit, "Tonight We Need a Lover").

" 'Cause when I go through her, it's just like a hot knife through butter" (Kiss).

"Squealing in passion as the rod of steel injects" (Judas Priest, in the top-forty song, "Eat Me Alive").

"My sister never made love to anyone else but me; incest is everything it is said to be" (Prince, in the solid-gold hit "Sister").

The lyrics to some groups, such as Nine Inch Nails and Marilyn Manson, are so sexually graphic and profane that we couldn't print them here. And much of the current rap music is filled with vulgar terms that degrade women and glamorize violence.

In an article in one teen magazine, Blacy Lawless of the band W.A.S.P. said, "I like to drink blood out of a skull and torture females on stage." In another, Elvis Costello said, "Rock and Roll is about sex, and I'm here to corrupt the youth of America."

This perverted, profane, degenerated blitz against kids' minds has been the worst mass attack ever made against our youth, an onslaught that rages with weapons that search the limits of depravity: Elton John singing of girls having sex with girls in "All the Young Girls Love Alice" . . . Alice Cooper singing of sex with a corpse in "Cold Ethyl" . . . Gene Simmons of Kiss talking in *Rock* magazine about "cycles and whips . . . all the things little girls dream about" . . . Pink Floyd's song "Sheep," opening with the Twenty-third Psalm then turning into blasphemy, echoing so many other songs that portray Satan as nothing to be feared and casting doubt on God's goodness.

Every day, one study revealed, more than 85 percent of American teenagers listen to popular rock music for at least two hours. That adds up to at least seventy-five thousand songs heard by each of these kids during his or her teenage years.

Another survey indicated that parents spend an average of thirty to ninety seconds a day in one-on-one, face-to-face communication with their teenage children. If those kids are getting hundreds of times more verbal input from rock and media stars . . . then guess whose behavior they'll copy?

Don't you think it's time to close the zoo?

Something Better

Our dog, Champ, taught me another encouraging truth about my home. If he had a dangerous chicken bone or sharp steak bone in his mouth, no act of Congress or California earthquake could make him give it up. But if I offered him a juicy piece of lean meat in the palm of my hand, then like any dog, he'd drop that bone every time.

Are you worried about the attraction some tantalizing but dangerous "bones" might hold for your kids? Then turn your home into a king's cut of prime rib to entice their taste buds. Make life at home a celebration for them—a homecoming party every evening after school and a holiday every weekend.

"The best way to make kids good," Oscar Wilde said, "is to keep them happy." Kids love to stay home when the home has parent leaders who make it the "funnest" place to be.

A picture I saw on a giant billboard years ago on I-40 continues to stay in mind. A family of five was holding hands and walking together, smiling. Big colorful letters read, "Get your good times together."

If you're concerned about all those quarters your children feed into video games, or the thousands of hours they spend in front of the TV, or how hard it is to get everyone to sit down together for a family dinner because the kids can't wait to go out with their friends . . . then get your good times together. The chances are excellent that you'll find your family closer than ever in the years ahead.

I haven't listened to a secular radio station more than once or twice a year since our first baby was born. The record companies would go out of business if our family's habits were contagious enough. Hollywood would have the nation's highest unemployment rate if my kids set the trends.

But we played in our home like a bunch of monkeys. Our house was rowdy, fun, creative, exciting, crazy. Did we missing anything? Maybe. Were our kids sheltered? Maybe. But would I trade a hilarious, tense, competitive game of good old Monopoly for an hour of filth and violence on TV? No way.

Is there life after television?

You bet!

What else can a family do together? For starters, try a few of these:

- Homemade carnivals in the living room, with prizes for the winner in each event: throwing darts at balloons, pitching pennies, tossing a hat on a broomstick, bobbing for apples
- Homemade miniature golf
- Balloon volleyball over a king-size bed
- Pillow fights
- Table games
- Puzzles
- Charades
- Coloring contests
- Making popcorn balls or caramel apples
- Leather or wood crafts
- Family baseball, football, volleyball (We always handicapped the better athletes to keep the competition close.)
- BB gun contests
- Bow and arrow competitions to see who can pop the most balloons
- Shuffleboard
- Go-cart racing
- Rollerskating
- Window shopping
- Scavenger hunts at the mall

- Spoil Mommy Day
- Date Night with Dad (I tried to give each daughter a memorable date—as well as teach them how a girl should be treated by a guy—by opening the door for her, seating her, giving her preference, and talking about the love, admiration, and respect I have for their mom.)
- Hunting trips, fishing, camping, hiking, horseback riding, or mountain climbing.

My kids still think I'm nuts for the day we packed a picnic basket with a white tablecloth, china, and candlesticks for breakfast at McDonald's.

Lord, Make Me Creative!

The first requirement for being a creative, contagious family leader is to develop a happy heart. Maintaining a cheerful spirit is a constant challenge for me, as it is for most parents who face so many pressures both inside and outside the home. It dampens even the hearts that want to be happy. The solution that works best for me—and I believe it's the key to being admired by your kids as a happy person—is to be continually thankful for all you have.

I find the easiest days to be happy are those when I wake up counting the thousands of blessings I have. "Thank you, Lord, for giving me life! The sun is up again—what a fantastic day! Thank you, God. . . . Thank you for Debbie-Jo—what a super wife! . . . Thank you for such neat kids—for Jamie, Corky, Brady, and Cooper. . . . And thank you for the forgiveness you've given me, and for the hope I have because I know you." The smile begins to grow. The day brightens. And when the pressures come later in the day, I shoot thank you arrows at them.

The second key to making your home a place for winning relationships is to take time every day to create fun and meaningful times together as a family. Yes, you can do it. As a friend who played professional football once said, "I'm through with all the negative self-talk I've been feeding myself about my not being creative. I'm going to ask God to make me creative and to take the role of creative leadership in my family!" With the same attitude, you'll succeed. There are a million ways to be creative.

Early one Saturday morning, when the kids were small, they were up watching cartoons on TV. Debbie-Jo had put in a tough week, so while she slept, I tiptoed out of the bedroom and joined the kids. After about ten minutes of watching them be mesmerized by an animated space movie, I was ready to make something happen.

We got a crazy idea, and within ten minutes it was in full bloom. Twelve feet of butcher paper, a handful of magic markers, four pint-sized children, and an inartistic father were sprawled across the living room floor making a giant "We Love You, Mommy" banner. We each took a section and scribbled like crazy. Each letter became a unique work of personal art. I wish you could have seen Debbie-Jo when she walked into her day of celebration!

Look back into your childhood for the good memories, and you'll smile at the times your mom or dad did something crazy or fun to make the family laugh. We need more of that today.

Use your creativity not only to make home a fun place but also to solve critical problems. I once worked closely with a seventeen-year-old boy who couldn't quit drinking—which, as is typical, led to lying and other problems. After a lot of fruitless discussions with him, I said, "I tell you what. If you'll give up your booze for a year, I'll quit drinking soft drinks for a year." He knew how much I enjoy a Dr. Pepper on a hot day.

After six months, his habit was broken—and he felt good about himself.

More Family Fun Ideas

A "love bombardment" works especially well with children eight years old and older. Have the family sit in a circle on the floor or around the table. Have each family member give an earnest, sincere compliment to a designated person in the circle. The person receiving the compliments may only listen and say, "Thank you." After that person has been bombarded, go on to the next until everyone has been in the spotlight.

Make mealtimes a fun experience every day. Let Dad offer to take care of the next day's household chores for whomever contributes most to positive conversation over dinner.

Place a coin bank or jar in the center of the table, with the rule that anyone (including you) who makes a negative, grouchy, or critical remark must put in a quarter of his own money. At the end of a week or month, decide together on a worthy cause to give the money to.

Clear the table after supper and have everyone sit an equal distance from each other, with chins resting just above the tabletop, ready to blow. Place a Ping-Pong ball in the center of the table. Whoever lets the ball drop gets put on the kitchen clean-up crew for the night. (Keep going till everyone gets to help.)

Family Goal Setting

Set aside a regular family night each week, and guard it from conflicts with anything else in everyone's schedule. Use the first one for family goal setting. Everyone pitches in ideas about what he or she would like to see the family accomplish. (An important rule: positive comments only.)

Clarify and organize your agreed-upon goals, then write down specific ways to accomplish each one, including a measurable plan of evaluation.

Following is a list of goals that our family came up with.

Goal #1: Have regular family devotions.

Method of accomplishment: A five-minute devotional time together each morning before breakfast. Everyone will take a turn being the leader.

Evaluation: "Excellent"—seven days a week, everyone present. "Good"—at least four days a week, and no more than one absence. "Poor"—less than four days a week, or more than one absence.

Goal #2: Pray together regularly as a family, apart from meal-times.

Method of accomplishment: We all meet at 9 P.M. for conversational prayer together.

Evaluation: Same as for family devotions.

Goal #3: Memorize Scripture together.

Method of accomplishment: Memorize three verses weekly, learning and discussing them during our other times together.

Evaluation: "Excellent"—three verses learned per week. "Good"— two verses learned per week. "Poor"—only one verse (or none) learned per week.

Use one family night each month to discuss, reevaluate, and redirect your efforts on family goals. You also can use these times together to look at budgets, schedules, and vacation plans. Another family night could be devoted to brainstorming ideas for fun activities together. After you list all the ideas mentioned, each person can secretly rate them on paper, using a one-to-ten rating scale. Collect the papers and start with the activities that get the highest score. If a questionable activity (such as seeing an R-rated movie) is suggested, just ask the question, "How would this fit into our family's spiritual or moral goals?"

I strongly encourage you, in your position of leadership in your family, to set and seek to carry out family goals. Effective leaders in any field always possess two main qualities: (1) They know where they are going; and (2) they let others participate in their vision and persuade them to go with them. Know where you want to go as a family, and—through genuine love and joy—get everyone else in your family to get there with you by defining and pursuing your goals.

A New Game

The hardest times for me to do something creative and fun with my family—when I often ended up settling for a wasted evening in front of the tube—was when I tried too hard to dream up something new and different. But one year my two boys and I struck a gold mine. We invented a game called "Climb & Rappel." Planning it took about half a day, but the game lasted all year!

The game was a takeoff of the children's game called "Chutes and Ladders," which has a game board with numbered squares interconnected by "ladders" that give you shortcuts to go forward and "chutes" that send you back. In our version, the game board represented a mountain, and the squares were labeled with numbers that correspond to a numbered list of special things to do with Daddy or Mommy.

To make your own version of the game, start by creating a game board on a large piece of poster paper, marking off a hundred or so numbered squares. (You can model it after the game board shown at the end of this chapter; or, if you have access to a photocopier with enlarging capabilities, simply copy the model board.) Our family's design included "climb" and "rappel" squares. When you landed on a "climb" square, you jumped up the mountain the designated number of spaces. When you hit a "rappel" square you went back down the distance indicated.

Place your finished board on the family room wall or on the refrigerator or in some other prominent place at home. Let each child in the family select a thumbtack or penny or magnet to serve as his or her token to move on the board.

Next, post your numbered list of "creative parent/kid events"—several dozen things you and your kids like to do together. (For examples, see our family's list at the end of this chapter.) Have a special privilege reserved for when a player reaches the final square on the board.

It should take weeks or even months of fun to get there. Each day, or maybe three days a week, when the time comes for those golden minutes together, have your children roll the dice and move their tokens that number of spaces on the game board. Whatever number they land on, go to the event list and do that event together.

When we played, my kids couldn't wait to come home from school each afternoon to roll the dice and see what we got to do together next.

'Cause You Were There

One beautiful spring day years ago, I was tied up at the office until dark. My youngest "round and firm and fully packed" boy had his best friend over, and they romped and played G.I. Joe for hours. Boy, were they having fun!

I dragged into the house just before bedtime and picked up my happy boy, told him he was a champ, and bounced him like a basketball into the bed two or three times. It must have lasted all of ten seconds. Then it was time to brush his teeth, put on his PJs, and hit the sack.

As I tucked him in, I asked, "What was the highlight of your day today, Cooper?" I thought I'd hear tall tales of soldiers at war. He looked me straight in the eye and said, "Getting bounced in bed."

"Really?" I asked, half shocked. "Why is that?"

He sunk in the truth: "'Cause you were there, Daddy . . . 'cause you were there."

I'd rather be a daddy than anything I know.

Closing the zoo each day gave me lots of opportunities.

Mommy and Daddy/Kid Events

For the
"Climb & Rappel" Game

1. Go to Mr. B's for an ice cream cone with Mommy or Daddy.
2. Identify five trees with Mommy.
3. Make homemade ice cream blizzard using a favorite candy bar, with Daddy.
4. Play Frisbee golf to Grandma's and back with Daddy.
5. Direct and videotape a family skit with Mommy.
6. Shoot three balloons in archery with Daddy.
7. Write an "I Love You" letter to an aunt or uncle with Mommy and Daddy.
8. Do the supper dishes with Daddy.
9. Go see Joey and Jeanie's new baby with Mommy.
10. Play a game of Sorry with Mommy and Daddy.
11. Take Chuck for a walk down by the lake with Daddy.
12. Do ten pull-ups with Mommy.
13. Make Papa's pancakes for breakfast with Daddy.
14. Jog to Cougar Trails and back with Mommy.
15. Memorize two new verses in John 1 with Daddy.
16. Call G. G. and C. C. with Mommy.
17. Do a finger painting with Daddy.
18. Go for a free swim at C of O with Mommy.
19. Go with Daddy to McDonald's for French fries.
20. With help from Daddy, lead family devotion tomorrow on Romans 6:1–2.

21. Read Archie comics to Mommy.
22. Make a modeling clay dinosaur with Mommy.
23. Go with Daddy to see Kris and Diane's new baby.
24. Write an "I Love You" letter with Daddy to a former camp counselor or babysitter.
25. Have a go-cart race with Mommy.
26. Shoot fifty points with BB gun with Daddy.
27. Play a Bozo game with brother or sister and Mommy.
28. With Daddy's help, set up a family picture with everyone in costume.
29. Visit Pardner with Daddy, and tell her three nice things you see.
30. Make a batch of chocolate chip cookies, and go with Daddy to take half of them to a favorite neighbor family.
31. Play home-run derby (until ten home runs are hit) in the gym with Mommy.
32. Have a tallest building competition in building blocks with Daddy.
33. Go with Mommy to McDonald's for a hot fudge sundae.
34. Play four games of Skee-Ball with Daddy.
35. Take a thirty-minute walk in the woods with Mommy.
36. Go with Daddy to see Brad and Debbie's new baby.
37. Go down and back on the monkey bars with Mommy.
38. Play a game of Crazy Eights with Daddy.
39. Go with Mommy to visit Grandma and Pappy.
40. Have a field practice in baseball with a brother or sister and Daddy.
41. Go fishing with Daddy.
42. Tour K-4 with Daddy, and tell Pappy ten new things you see.
43. Hit fifty tennis balls with Mommy.
44. Do twenty push-ups with Daddy.
45. Go to Wal-Mart with Mommy and buy something special.
46. Play nine holes of mini-golf with Daddy.
47. Shoot the 410 with Mommy.
48. Play catch-and-step-back using a tennis ball with Daddy. (Play until you catch ten in a row.)

49. Do a video production with Mommy for grandparents.
50. Shoot five hidden balloons in the trees using BB gun with Daddy.
51. Go with Daddy to McDonald's for breakfast.
52. Watch *Noah's Ark* or another Bible video with Mommy.
53. Go to the Christian bookstore with Daddy and buy a gift for Mommy.
54. Play soccer ball keep-away with Daddy.
55. Call Pardner with Mommy, and talk for at least two minutes.
56. Write a letter of appreciation to a teacher or Bob Abbott with Daddy.
57. Take Chuck on a walk to K-4 with Mommy.
58. With Daddy's help, plan the devotional for tomorrow morning.
59. Do twenty seat-drops on the trampoline with Daddy.
60. Go roller-skating with Mommy.
61. (You make one up.)
62. Take three photographs for the scrapbook with Daddy.
63. Go to the park in Branson with Mommy.
64. "Father Abraham" with Daddy.
65. With volleyball, do throws and catches with Daddy.
66. Make a cassette tape for G. G. and C. C. with Mommy.
67. Shoot ten basketballs lay-ups with Daddy.
68. Shoot arrows from the balcony to the football field with Daddy.
69. Play hopscotch at Kanakomo with Mommy.
70. With Daddy, make a crayon portrait of Mommie and write "I Love You" on it.
71. Do ten front flips on the trampoline with Mommy.
72. Dribble and shoot ten goals in soccer with Daddy.
73. Tie four different rope knots with Daddy.
74. Play checkers with Mommy.
75. Set up a putt-putt game around the house and play with Daddy.
76. Ride bikes in the K-Dome with Mommy.
77. Watch a Disney video with Mommy.
78. Let Daddy bounce you on the trampoline.
79. (You make one up.)

80. Play around-the-world in basketball with Mommy.
81. Do twenty throws and catches using baseball and glove with Daddy.
82. Go canoeing in Tarzanland with Mommy.
83. Set a trout line in slough with Daddy.
84. Break balloons with bow and arrows with Mommy.
85. Play shuffleboard with Daddy.
86. Have a paper airplane contest with Mommy—grand finale off the balcony.
87. Go to Christian bookstore with Daddy and buy a gift for Grandma.
88. Do twenty football throws and catches with Daddy.
89. Break three balloons with bow and arrows with Daddy.
90. Write a letter of appreciation to the postmaster, sheriff, or police chief with Mommy.
91. Play "Pig" in basketball with Mommy.
92. (You make one up.)
93. Go to Pardner's with Daddy and ride the wagon around the circle.
94. Do twenty baseball throws and catches with Mommy.
95. With Daddy, take two photographs for gifts to grandparents.
96. Do twenty football throws and catches with Daddy.
97. Play checkers with Daddy.
98. Tumble (Caw-Caw) in the living room with Daddy.
99. Go fishing with Mommy.
100. Do twenty push-ups with Daddy.

CLIMB & RAPPEL

TOP

	100	99	

| | 96 | 97 | RAPPEL 5 spaces ▼ | 98 | |

| 95 | 94 | 93 | 92 | 91 | 90 |

| 83 | 84 | RAPPEL 4 spaces ▼ | 85 | 86 | 87 | 88 | 89 |

| 82 | 81 | 80 | 79 | 78 | RAPPEL 2 spaces ▼ | ▲ CLIMB 2 spaces | 77 |

| 71 | 72 | 73 | RAPPEL 4 spaces ▼ | ▲ CLIMB 2 spaces | 74 | 75 | 76 |

| 70 | RAPPEL 7 spaces ▼ | 69 | 68 | 67 | 66 | 65 | 64 |

| 57 | 58 | 59 | 60 | 61 | ▲ CLIMB 1 space | 62 | 63 |

| 56 | 55 | ▲ CLIMB 4 spaces | 54 | 53 | 52 | 51 | 50 |

| 43 | 44 | 45 | 46 | RAPPEL 2 spaces ▼ | 47 | 48 | 49 |

| 42 | 41 | RAPPEL 2 spaces ▼ | 40 | ▲ CLIMB 3 spaces | 39 | 38 | 37 |

| 29 | 30 | 31 | 32 | 33 | 34 | 35 | 36 |

| 28 | ▲ CLIMB 4 spaces | 27 | 26 | 25 | 24 | RAPPEL 2 spaces ▼ | 23 |

| 16 | 17 | 18 | ▲ CLIMB 7 spaces | 19 | 20 | 21 | 22 |

| 15 | 14 | 13 | 12 | 11 | ▲ CLIMB 4 spaces | 10 | 9 |

| 1 | 2 | 3 | 4 | 5 | 6 | 7 | 8 |

test \ test \ n. 1. A trial that determines your true grit. 2. A set of questions whose answers reveal depth and honesty.

6

Test Yourself

I like to see a man proud of the place in which he lives. I like to see a man live so that his place will be proud of him.
—ABRAHAM LINCOLN

Hands build a house; hearts build a home.

In the past, I've had my wife, my closest employees, and my children evaluate my performance as a husband, a boss, and a dad. Boy, was I awakened! I didn't know so many blind spots were possible for a man with twenty-twenty vision, but it's been one of the most productive experiences of my life.

People with responsibility—corporate presidents, coaches, committee leaders, parents—want to know on occasion how they're doing. They can ask their peers and get a fraction of the answer. They can ask their supervisors and get another partial picture. But if they ask those who report to them, they'll get a real eye-opener!

That's why I've supplied a suggested evaluation (in the last half of this chapter) for your school-age kids. It's a "Relationship Inventory" to be completed candidly by each one to help you know how well you're doing as a parent. The questions have been shaped through the input of a number of teenagers who've taken the test.

Make a copy of the Relationship Inventory for each of your children over five years old. A child under age nine should be assisted by a trusted adult (other than a parent) in completing the inventory, and children ages nine to thirteen may also want some help. A teenager will probably do best completing it alone.

Assure your children that there are no "wrong" answers and that the more they open up their hearts to reveal their true feelings, the more helpful it will be to you. Let your children know that you are humble and eager to learn.

If possible, parents should work together in reviewing the answers and computing the score. After the inventory has been completed by each child . . .

1. Add up all the numbers circled.
2. Divide the total you got in step 1 by the number of questions the child answered (if the child answered every question, that number is 21).
3. Round off the total from step 2 to the nearest whole number, and mark the result on this scale:

1   2   3   4   5   6   7   8   9   10
very poor   very good

If your score is high . . . keep showing your children love, encouragement, and support; keep being creative; and keep praying. Don't stop growing, but strive to get even better!

If your score is not as high as you had expected or would like, I hope you'll really pull yourself into the content of this book and seek to expand on every constructive idea that it spurs in your mind. Be open to new directions in your family life, and redouble your energies spent in relationships at home.

If your score is quite low, I would encourage you to also consider getting a well-trained counselor to talk with you and your children. (A caution here: Be sure to find someone dedicated to the authority of God's Word. A lot of the secular child psychology that is available and popular today is as destructive as it is expensive.)

Regardless of your score, carefully review your children's answers to each question, and talk with your children about them, especially the questions on which you scored lowest. As you respond to touchy areas, don't kick over the beehive by being condemning or judgmental. Be thankful that your children have been open and honest about their disappointments in their relationships with you.

You're likely to be walking on tender ground as you review and discuss these answers . . . but consider this picture:

A farmer waits all winter for the warming spring days when he can get the plow out of his barn and break the soil for planting. The sharp, heavy steel of the plow is necessary to cut through the crust that has been hardening since the harvest months ago. The earth must be broken and ready before the seeds—little seeds packed with potential, representing the farmer's future livelihood—can be sown.

In every family there are layers of insensitivity . . . hardening crusts that hide crucial needs in parent-child relationships. This inventory may well have been a sharp, cutting plow that cut through the crust and exposed those needs—perhaps painfully.

But say welcome to springtime! With the soil broken and ready, it's time to plant seeds of love and commitment and encouragement, seeds that will bear an unimaginably good harvest when the growing season ends.

Relationship Inventory

A Survey of Your Feelings about Your Dad and Mom

Directions: Each numbered statement that follows is an incomplete sentence. Below each statement—on each end of a scale of numbers—are two phrases that could be used to complete the sentence in very different ways.

Think about how you would complete the sentence so that it reflects how you feel. Circle the number on the scale that shows best where you are in your attitudes and evaluation.

If you feel a question doesn't apply to your situation, skip it and go on to the next one.

1. In the eyes of my dad, I see myself as . . .

1	2	3	4	5	6	7	8	9	10
insignificant, unimportant									extremely valuable

2. In the eyes of my mom, I see myself as . . .

1	2	3	4	5	6	7	8	9	10
insignificant, unimportant									extremely valuable

3. In the eyes of others my age who know me, I see myself as . . .

1	2	3	4	5	6	7	8	9	10
insignificant, unimportant									extremely valuable

4. If my father had something very important to do at his job and at the same time I really needed him, I feel that typically he would . . .

1   2   3   4   5   6   7   8   9   10
first take care of his work   drop everything to spend time with me

5. If my mother had something very important to do at her job and at the same time I really needed her, I feel that typically she would . . .

1   2   3   4   5   6   7   8   9   10
first take care of his work   drop everything to spend time with me

6. I feel my mom and dad love each other . . .

1   2   3   4   5   6   7   8   9   10
not at all   very, very, very much

7. The amount of love I feel in my heart from God is . . .

1   2   3   4   5   6   7   8   9   10
nonexistent   extremely high

8. The amount of love I feel in my heart for God is . . .

1   2   3   4   5   6   7   8   9   10
nonexistent   extremely high

9. After I do something special (such as create or build something original or score an especially good grade on a big test at school) and come home and tell about it, my mom or dad probably will . . .

1   2   3   4   5   6   7   8   9   10
pay no attention   stop everything and show excitement—and even tell other people about it

10. When my mom or dad is occupied with something and I interrupt to say I have an important question, usually she or he will . . .

1   2   3   4   5   6   7   8   9   10
pay no attention to me   stop immediately and give me undivided attention

11. It seems to me that, when it comes to his family or his other interests (such as his work, his friends, or his hobbies), my dad's number-one priority is . . .

1   2   3   4   5   6   7   8   9   10
his own interests   his family

12. It seems to me that, when it comes to her family or her other interests (such as her work, her friends, or her hobbies), my mom's number-one priority is . . .

1   2   3   4   5   6   7   8   9   10
her own interests   her family

13. I feel as if my dad knows the "real me" . . .

1   2   3   4   5   6   7   8   9   10
not at all   very, very well

14. I feel as if my mom knows the "real me" . . .

1   2   3   4   5   6   7   8   9   10
not at all   very, very well

15. When I need advice and guidance, I go to one or both of my parents . . .

1   2   3   4   5   6   7   8   9   10
never   always

16. When I am hurting, I go to one or both of my parents . . .

1   2   3   4   5   6   7   8   9   10
never   always

17. Someday, when I raise my own kids, I will do it . . .

1   2   3   4   5   6   7   8   9   10
totally different from   just like I was raised
the way I was raised

18. I feel my overall relationship with my dad is . . .

   1   2   3   4   5   6   7   8   9   10
very distant   very close

19. I feel my overall relationship with my mom is . . .

   1   2   3   4   5   6   7   8   9   10
very distant   very close

20. If I were to take this same survey a year from now, I would like to be able to rate my overall relationship with my dad like this:

   1   2   3   4   5   6   7   8   9   10
very distant   very close

21. If I were to take this same survey a year from now, I would like to be able to rate my overall relationship with my mom like this:

   1   2   3   4   5   6   7   8   9   10
very distant   very close

After thinking about these last two answers, write down one or two creative ideas that you believe would help you achieve the relationship level you desire with your mom, your dad, or both:

And finally, write down two ways in which you believe your mom or dad (or both) could help you achieve that kind of relationship.

counselor \cown-se-lur\ n. 1. Someone who has per-fected the art of listening.

7

Unconditional Listening, Unconditional Love

It's hard to believe that a relationship can
last when you've never seen one.
—OLIVIA NEWTON-JOHN

"I have a problem," a teenager says (in word or action).
"What is it?" we ask.

"I want to run away," the teen says.

The typical adult response: "That's crazy! You'd never make it out there."

"Well, I'm going to do it anyway," the teenager says. "I think I can make it."

Wanting to run away is not this teenager's problem. The wise parent —with listening ears, a loving heart, an understanding mind, and the foundation of a relationship built on trust—can find the real source of trouble.

"I have a problem."

"What is it?"

"I want to run away."

"What's wrong?"

"Nobody cares."

"I care. Can you tell me what you're feeling?"

"I just feel so confused."

"What about?"

"I feel so guilty."

"Can you tell me more? I really want to help you. I've been there—I've wrestled with guilt myself."

I'm not a professional counselor, but I've learned (*wow*—have I learned!) that listening is the central ingredient in good counseling. The most valuable thirty minutes in my entire education took place in a small seminar with my colleague and great friend David Stone. He taught me an effective, simple method of listening—simple enough that it takes only thirty minutes to learn. Any patient parent can use it with a hurting child. It gives amazing results, especially when used with teenagers.

I've been blown away watching the constructive process this method leads to in a teenager's moment of confusion. If I could encourage parents to learn and apply thoroughly only one communication technique, this would be it.

When your child comes to you seeking help with a serious problem or concern and you want a way to tenderly but thoroughly discuss it, try this approach: Tell him or her you want to ask only three questions, but you would like to repeat them several times, and each time you do, you want a different answer. Tell your child that your goal is simply to help him or her discover the proper solution and work toward applying it.

For the method to work effectively, you must follow three important ground rules.

First, you must provide an atmosphere of empathy—with your eyes, your facial expressions, and your words. The child needs to see and hear you saying, "I want to understand what you're going through. I care for you, and I'm eager to help you get to the heart of what's troubling you."

Second, don't jump to conclusions and give premature advice. The surface problem (drinking, fighting, curfew-breaking, disrespect, or whatever) is a result of the real problem that lies much deeper in the child's heart. Keep asking questions and *listen* to uncover the real problem.

Third, don't condemn or criticize. Your negative response will stop the process quicker than anything.

The lead-off question in this method is, *"What's wrong?"* Or, *"What do you want?"* You're trying to find out what's going on in the teenager's head.

Follow that with, *"What are you feeling?"* Here you're trying to discover what's going on in his or her heart. In this second stage of uncovering emotions, you can *chase* the basic question with another to help identify the feeling more clearly. For example, you ask, "How are you feeling?" and the child answers, "I feel sad." You could then say, "What's the sadness?" The response might be, "I just feel so hurt, so rejected."

Next, ask, *"What are you doing about that problem?"* Or, *"What are you going to do about it?"* When the child answers, don't draw conclusions. Bite your tongue when you want to give advice. Instead, start over again with the lead-off question, so you can sift down further to the real problem.

Be sure to kindly demand a different answer each go-round to each of the three questions. After a few minutes of patient questioning and active listening, you'll sense that the child truly sees an action he or she needs to take. At this advantageous moment, you can ask, "What do you need to do now to solve that problem?" Wait patiently for the answer. When it comes, ask, "Are you willing to do that? Will you come tell me how it's going after you do it?"

Learn to listen! Learn to ask questions! As you help the teenager uncover the emotional mess that so often hides the real problem, you can help him or her commit to solving it.

Below are examples of how I've used the technique in counseling teens. (In each example, the teenager's words are in italics.)

Abortion Scars—Polly

"What's wrong?"

"I'm really hurting bad."

"How do you feel?"

"Terrible."

"What are you doing?"

"Talking to you."

"What's wrong?"

"I'm just so awful."

"How do you feel?"

"Sad."

"What's the sadness?"

"I don't know. Things are so bad, I cry every day."

"What are you doing?"

"I don't know what to do."

(Now the layers begin to peel off.)

"What's wrong?"

"I killed my baby. I killed him. I had an abortion last month and I feel so terrible. And he said that he loved me, but now he hates me. He said, 'I thought it would bring us closer together, but now . . .' "

(She begins to sob. I comfort her and wait patiently to proceed.)

"Polly, how are you feeling?"

"Terrible—so wrong."

"What are you doing?"

"I can't talk to anyone about it."

"No one?"

"Well, my parents won't listen. They're always mad at me, and all they do is yell at me when I try to talk to them."

(The temptation is to stop here and begin to give advice—for example, about not having premarital sex. But having sex is not Polly's main problem. It's deeper than that. I find that many guys and girls who have been part of an abortion experience continue to be sexually active because there's something missing deep inside them.)

"What's wrong?"

"I just hate myself—I've hated myself for so long."

"How do you feel?"

"Mad at myself. Why can't I do what's right?"

"What are you doing now?"

"I'm listening now."

(She looks up at me.)

"What do you want, Polly?"

"I want to like myself."

"How do you feel?"

"Torn up inside."

"What are you doing?"

"I'm confused."

"What's wrong?"

"I'm not being me. I've turned into someone I hate."

"Who is the person you really want to be?"

"I don't know."

(I recognize the cop out and chase it.)

"Don't know, Polly, or just won't say?"

"Well, I don't want to get drunk and stuff."

"What are you doing to be the person you want to be?"

"I don't know what to do."

(Another cop out.)

"Don't know, or just won't do it?"

"Well . . ."

(At this point I open both my hands. I refer to my right hand as the real Polly that she wants to be, deep down inside, and to my left hand as the fake Polly that is making her so miserable.)

"Which of these do you really want to be?"

"I want to be the girl God wants me to be."

"What are you doing?"

"I don't know."

"Polly, what do you need to do to get what you want?"

"I need to give my life to Christ. I need to feel his love . . . get forgiven . . . you know, ask him into my life."

This went on for quite a while. I continued to refer to the right and left hand when she'd throw up cop outs like, "It's so hard." I kept her focusing on what she wanted more than anything else. Finally she found it!

Attempted Suicide—Kathy

"What do you want?"

"To be accepted."

"How do you feel?"

"Sad."

"What's the sadness?"

"Sorta lonesome, I guess."

"What are you doing?"

"It doesn't work. I've tried and nothing works."

"What do you want?

"To gain my daddy's love."

"How do you feel?"

"I feel sad."

"You said that already. Can you think of a different answer?"

"Tired. Tired of trying."

"What are you doing?"

"I can't do anything. They find fault with everything I do."

"What do you want? What would really make you happy right now?"

"To make them happy."

"How do you feel?"

"Frustrated. I feel like a failure."

"What are you doing?"

"Nothing really."

"What do you want?"

"I want to be satisfied that I've done good."

"How do you feel?"

"Nobody notices when I do something right. They expect too much from me. They don't see the good things."

"What are you doing?"

"Praying."

"About what?"

"For strength to be able to talk to them again."

"What do you want?"

"I want to get along with my parents and have them as friends."

"How do you feel?"

"Frustrated, confused—you see, they're so condemning. They expect me to be perfect, and when I make a mistake, they come down really hard on me."

"What are you doing?"

"Trying to share with them."

"Trying?"

"It's hard."

"What do you want?"

"I know . . ."

"What do you need to do, Kathy?"

"Tell them . . ."

"Tell them what?"

"Let them know I appreciate them."

"How?"

"Thank them."

"How?"

"Do something."

"What?"

"Start all over."

"How?"

"I guess . . ."

"Guess?"

"I have to forget the past. (She cries softly.) Forgive them. I have to get rid of my negative attitude."

"How?"

"Focus on positive things."

At this point we made a list of all the positive qualities she found in her father, and I talked to her about how important it was to focus on the good qualities in people you love. We prayed together to begin the forgiveness process, and she went away feeling a sense of hope.

I couldn't wait to spend time with her parents. The opportunity came a week later. After I helped them realize a few things they were doing to injure their daughter's self-esteem, the family was ready to put things back together again.

I Can't Say I Love You—Bill

After spending three weeks with uplifting people in an atmosphere of fun and happiness, I came back to camp and encountered Bill. At age fourteen, he faced a life of never-ending depression. He came to me with a scowl fixed firmly on his face.

"*I've got a problem . . . I'm so down.*"

"What's wrong?"

"*I don't know.*"

"Is it camp?"

"*I don't think so.*"

"Is it your counselor?"

"*Nah.*"

"Bill, I'm going to take you through a little process that I think might help you." (I carefully explained the three-question process, and he agreed to give it a try.)

"What's wrong?"

"*I'm just not excited about anything.*"

"How do you feel?"

"*Confused.*"

"What's the confusion?"

"*I just feel messed up inside.*"

"What are you doing?"

"*Nothing. I don't know what to do.*"

"What's wrong?"

(Bill begins to frown. There is a long pause.)

"*I just feel something missing—missing inside.*"

"How do you feel?"

"*All empty.*"

"What's the emptiness?"

"*I don't know. Kind of lonely, I guess.*"

"What are you doing?"

"*Not much.*"

"What's wrong?"

"*I'm not looking forward to seeing my parents, and I know I ought to be.*"

"How do you feel?"

"*Lost.*"

"What are you doing?"

"*What do you mean?*"

"You say you feel lost; what are you doing to keep from feeling that way?"

"*Hmmm . . .*"

"What's wrong?"

"*I can't tell them I love them.*"

"How do you feel?"

"*Sad.*"

"What's the sadness?"

"*I want to tell them I love them. I just can't.*"

(Here again—as with Polly—is a cop out that needs chasing.)

"Can't or won't?"

"*Well . . .*" (Long pause.)

"What's wrong?"

"*I haven't told them I love them in so long.*" (He begins to cry.)

"How do you feel?"

"*Really bad.*"

"What are you doing?"

"*Nothing.*"

(It's time, I feel, to ask the pointed question.)

"What do you need to do, Bill?"

"*Write—I need to tell them I love them.*"

"When do you need to do it?"

"Today!"

"Will you?"

"Yes, I will." (A big smile appears on his face.)

"Will you come talk to me after you've written them?"

"Yes."

Bill took off excitedly to get his pen and paper.

The next day Bill came to me with another smile: "Wow," he said. "How can something so little affect you in such a big, big way?"

Unconditional Love

I eagerly anticipated meeting Bill's parents when they came to visit him near the end of his camp session. When the day came, he realized why he'd had such a hard time expressing his love to them. I told his parents what a fine boy he was and how much he had learned during his time at camp.

"He needed to," his dad blurted out. I gulped.

The next day Bill won the fifty-yard dash in a camp track meet. Afterward I went over to where his parents were sitting in lawn chairs under a shade tree. "Did you see Bill's race?" I asked excitedly. "He won his entire division!"

"Well, he should have," his dad said. I gulped again.

The only compliment for Bill I got out of them in the three days we were together was, "Well, he's a good athlete."

Both Bill and Kathy had missed out on the full experience of unconditional parental love. They are just two of the many kids today who believe the love and acceptance they receive from their parents is based on performance or appearance—"I love your beautiful eyes." "I love you because you made straight A's." "I love you because you scored twelve points in last night's game." When they don't feel they're meeting the expected standards, they feel as if the love is gone.

A very accomplished sixteen-year-old athlete came to me one summer after a somebody-notice-me suicide attempt. After a great deal of listening and digging into the heart of her insecurity, I found the roots of it embedded in an over-demanding and temperamental parent. Two weeks later I carefully pointed out my observations to the parent, who protested, "But look at all her athletic accomplishments! She's the most motivated child in the family!"

"Yes sir," I agreed, "but do you know why she works so hard in her athletics?"

"No, not really," he replied.

"That's where she gets her pats on the back. She feels the only time she's appreciated is when she succeeds in sports."

In contrast to the narrow demands of performance-based love, unconditional love is creative and wide-ranging and rich in the response it breeds in the one being loved.

I'm the happy victim of seven cases of unconditional love. My parents really believe in me and hardly notice when I make a mistake. My wife has never demanded my performance for her love. My four children think they have the best daddy in the world, despite having front-row seats from which to view my shortcomings. This love has a powerful effect on me. First, it makes me happy and fulfilled. Second, it puts a burning desire in my heart to please them in every way! I don't want to let them down. I'll do anything to do right by them.

I had an eye-opening conversation with a girl who's a model of a well-rounded, responsible, moral teenager. She told me that her mom and dad communicated to her daily how proud they were of her and how much they respected her. Cindy told me she never wanted to disappoint such a great expression of love. "Even when I went away to college and lived on my own," she said, "I always tried to do the right thing. I couldn't stand the thought of letting my parents down. They always made me feel so loved."

I can't stress enough how much kids today need to see and hear and feel that unconditional love from their parents, over and over and over again. It's the pivotal need in their lives, and when it's received, it forms the apex of their hearts. It gives them the necessary strength and courage to face every pressure, day after day, for the rest of their lives.

I know in the depths of my heart that the committed love I enjoy from my parents reflects the unbreakable bond of my heavenly Father's love for me. I read in Romans 8:38–39 that nothing—absolutely nothing—can separate me from God's love in Christ Jesus our Lord. God had to go through a lot to back up that statement—and my parents had to go through a lot to back up their commitment as well.

My mom and dad have always lived each day to meet their children's needs, and I feel so fortunate to have grown up under such exceptional examples.

My mom is the total mother. She enjoyed meeting our needs to the maximum. As we were growing up, a little inscription thumbtacked to the kitchen wall read, "The best way for a mother to have time to herself is at night when she does the dishes."

When we were young, Daddy read books to us until it seemed like all the print was read off the pages. He made the best Uncle Remus you ever heard. With his deep Mississippi accent, his sound effects, and his imaginative gestures, he brought Brer Bear, Brer Rabbit, and Ol' Brer Fox right into our room.

At night he taught us to pray and gave us words of reassurance and encouragement to make bed a secure place to snuggle into. As we grew up and our needs began to change, he changed to meet them. In the middle of his career, he sacrificed to take on ownership of a summer camp, so we could grow up in that environment.

I had many heartbreaks in my growing up years, but Daddy was always there to pick me up when I fell. I'll never forget his love, acceptance, and words of wisdom the day I came home sobbing after finding out my best buddy had gotten a starting position on the football team and I was to sit on the bench. Later, as a tiny noseguard at Southern Methodist University, I got clobbered Saturday after heartbreaking Saturday. Daddy was always there. I grew to depend on seeing his kind and encouraging face outside the locker room after a game. He didn't care about the score. He cared about me.

I think the key to his serving love, which made him best friends with my two brothers and me, is the way he identified our unique needs (we're so different from each other!) and sought to meet them.

My brother Bob was a woodsman. Staring through a 30.06 Winchester scope at a ten-point whitetail buck was like Mardi Gras to Bob. He shot his first buck sitting in Daddy's lap at age nine. He shot his first moose, bear, duck, goose, and dove at various ages in various parts of the country but always with the same hunting buddy.

My brother Bill was Daddy's most "interesting" project. Bill gave my dad a taste of what was to come when he ran away on his tricycle. But Dad knew how to get Bill through all the scrapes he got into over the years: Stand by his side. Be there to help him find success in his projects. Keep him interested.

Well past retirement age, my dad continues to work daylight to dark, six and half days a week, to help us have happy and successful lives.

How about the kids in your life? Do they really feel loved by you? Do they feel they can depend on you to be there when they need you? Or do they feel they have to measure up to your expectations before they receive your approval?

The most famous teacher of all time spoke about how to become a great leader. His view was typically revolutionary and to the point: "If any one wants to be first, he shall be last of all, and servant of all" (Mark 9:35). His pupils recalled those famous words when they later found Him kneeling before them with a towel and bowl of water, washing their dirty feet the night before He was killed.

The greatness Jesus Christ promised for those who serve is reserved for those who give to give. The folks who give to get are traders, not givers, and they raise a family of traders to follow them.

Take time today to write down the names of your spouse and children. Beside each name, record some special deed you can do for that person—things you can do to meet your family's abundant needs for your time, your expressions of value for them, your hugs, and your encouragement.

Transformed Dodgers

Dave Stewart, a standout pitcher for nine years with the Los Angeles Dodgers, tells of a slump the team went through during his last season there. The team had won only twice in ten games. Their frustration finally reached a peak in a game with Cincinnati, which they led six to nothing only to lose eight to six.

The post-game locker room was gloomy. Manager Tommy Lasorda entered and sat down beside his players. After much hesitation, Lasorda simply looked around at the defeated faces and asked, "What's wrong?" Wisely, he said nothing more.

After a long silence, one normally quiet player spoke up and expressed with heart-baring openness his own struggles and disappointments. Others began one by one to talk, venting months of pent-up frustrations. Several players broke down and cried.

Lasorda simply continued to listen.

The nightmare was over . . . and the transformed Dodgers went on to win eleven of their next thirteen games.

forgiveness \for-giv-nes\ n. 1. Love's irresistible response to "I'm sorry." 2. Christlike pardon for thoughtlessness, haste, and cruelty. 3. An incomparable relief.

8

Which Way Are
You Facing?

You can't plow a straight row looking backward.
—TOM JOHNSON

The comic strip *Peanuts* often makes my day. What's amazing about these cartoons is what's amazing about life. Maybe someday Charles Schulz will win the Nobel "Family Peace" Prize for them.

One strip opened with Charlie Brown and Lucy, two heroes of plain human wit, aboard a luxury ocean liner. They were strolling on deck, and in the background were sunbathers in lounge chairs.

With his typically simple facial expression, Charlie says, "Lucy, some people's chairs face the back of the ship; they can only see where we've been."

He continues: "Some people's chairs face the side of the ship, and they can only see things as they go by."

"And some people's chairs face the ship's bow, and they see only what's ahead."

In the final frame he asks, "Lucy, which way is your chair facing today?"

A great question for Lucy—and for you and me as parents. *Which way are you facing today?*

Some parents like to pitch tents and camp out on their children's past failures. Or like the seagulls following ocean liners, they scavenge the garbage dumped overboard. In anyone's life, the view backward includes some unattractive scenes. I've dumped some garbage of my own along the way. So have my kids, whose debris has sometimes been accompanied by my own mistakes.

The closeknit families I'm around aren't made up of perfect kids or perfect parents. But they do have this in common: They're a team of professional forgivers.

The father who comes to me for relief and says, "You just don't know my son!" usually has a son who'll say to me, "You just don't know my dad!" I love to tell each that he's right but that I know someone who knows them both and loves them anyway. In fact, the one who knows them best also loves them the most.

It's amazing to think about . . . God the Creator, who knows and sees everything behind and alongside and in front of our ship as we sail through life, sometimes smoothly and sometimes with difficulty—our God is focused on our potential and forgives everything—*everything*— about our past.

So I don't have to invent forgiveness. I don't have to produce it, as the sun produces light and heat. Instead, I just want to become a full moon, reflecting toward my kids the same attitude that God shines on me. My kids love it. I love it. My doctor loves it. I sleep well at night that way.

In another *Peanuts* episode, Lucy is standing all alone in left field, mouth wide open, baseball glove thrust expectantly overhead. "I've got it!" she screams. In the second frame, she calls out again, "I've got it!" Then a third time she proclaims to her teammates with commanding confidence, "I've got it!" Next we see the ball drop to the ground without even touching her glove. Lucy stares at the ball, half-hidden in the grass. "I've been wrong a lot lately," she says.

I think she was trying to sum up my life. I, too, have been wrong a lot lately. Most of us have. We spend a lot of time thinking, "I've got it!" only to watch the ball gather more grass stains at our feet.

It's the same with our kids and always will be. So the question isn't about how many balls they will drop, how many times they will disappoint us, how many letdowns they will go through . . . but rather, how we will respond.

Which way are you facing?

A story has been handed down through the ages about a generous king who liked to help the most promising entrepreneurs of his kingdom by loaning them large sums of money for their business projects. One young businessman with grandiose plans borrowed a million dollars from the king. The project turned out to be more consuming than the young man had dreamed, so he borrowed another million—and continued borrowing even more from His Majesty. He used some of the borrowed money to support the extravagant lifestyle he had adopted along the way.

Soon the end was near. Bills were long past due. The man's business was bankrupt, his pockets empty, his credit rating shattered. All his magnificent possessions were taken away, and he and his family moved in with kind neighbors. In humiliation and dread, he awaited the day of reckoning before the king.

The summons came: His Royal Highness demanded to see this problem debtor.

Bowing before the ruler, the businessman pleaded in humble repentance for mercy. He promised that if his life were spared, he and his wife and children—and someday his grandchildren and great grandchildren—would go to work in one of the king's factories, generation after generation, until the debt was repaid.

The king was moved with compassion. He decided to employ an outrageous grace heretofore unknown in the history of his own land or of any surrounding kingdom. He would set the young man free. He himself would cover the multimillion-dollar debt. He announced his decision and dismissed the man to return to his family.

The sun seemed somehow brighter and the air so much sweeter as the young man skipped down the palace steps. *Now,* he thought, *by somehow pulling together a little cash, I can get a good start once again.*

Not far from the palace, he by chance encountered one of his former salesmen—who, the businessman quickly remembered, happened to owe him a thousand dollars, a debt that now was due. They exchanged greetings, and the salesman complimented the businessman on how well and refreshed he appeared. Then the businessman immediately inquired about the thousand dollars.

The salesman seemed to have trouble answering. The businessman's face reddened as the salesman spoke nervously about things being tight and unexpected expenses at home. With sudden rage, the businessman grabbed the salesman's collar and promised to have him and his family jailed if the debt wasn't repaid the following day.

During a sleepless night, the salesman called in his friends to share in his misery. Early the next morning, knowing the king's kindness and generosity, they hurried to the palace and requested to see His Majesty. When the audience was granted, they asked the king for a thousand-dollar loan to meet an urgent need, which they explained in full. They happened to mention as well the name of the salesman's creditor.

The king became furious. Before an hour had passed, he had the businessman arrested, questioned, and sentenced to life imprisonment.

When I consider how often I have failed miserably as a parent and contemplate the amazing grace I've been afforded by my heavenly Father, it really isn't difficult to forgive those tiny debts that are owned to me by one of my children or my wife. I can't forget the times I failed and had to ask God for mercy. I'll never forget . . .

> . . . the countless times I've come home after going somewhere with my family and gone to my room alone, sometimes with tears, realizing what a pitiful job I had done that day as a daddy.

> . . . the times I raised my voice toward my wife.

> . . . an unusually heated argument when I felt the urge to hit my wife. I'll be forever grateful I didn't yield to that urge. I

pleaded for God's control, since I realized my self-control was still immature and lacking.

Too many times I have failed to live out the sermons I preached to my kids!

With all the failures in my personal life, I make a conscious effort to focus on thoughts of gratitude to my heavenly Father, who came to earth in the person of His Son, Jesus Christ, to pay off the enormous debt I've incurred here.

I spent the first two and half decades of my life trying to climb the performance stepladder, in order to gain acceptance from God. When I realized the ladder was too short, I appealed to God's mercy to forgive my great debt. I began to see that my acceptance from God came from his grace alone. That's why I never get tired of Paul's words of security written to the early Christians living throughout Rome:

> For I am convinced that neither death, nor life, nor angels, nor principalities, nor things present, nor things to come, nor powers, nor height, nor depth, nor any other created thing, shall be able to separate us from the love of God, which is in Christ Jesus our Lord. (Rom. 8:38–39)

A few years ago, a dear friend of mine died. He should have lived a few more years, but a fire that consumed his residence of many years left him despondent. He never really recovered the will to live after walking away with only his pajamas from the only place he and his kids had ever called home.

Shortly after the fire, I telephoned my friend to console him in his grief. I asked him what his greatest loss was. He was a talented artist, so I thought he might describe a lost painting. Or perhaps the successful hunter in him would make him mention a favorite animal trophy destroyed in the blaze. He surprised me by saying he regretted most the loss of many spools of old family movies.

After reflection, I agree with his priorities. Beginning when I was a little boy, our family always spared a few dollars for filming home movies. They're a carnival to watch. My wife and I became regular users of videotape, and many a night we rolled on the floor laughing at Daddy's big nose and Mommy's crazy faces.

Last May, before Jamie's wedding, I literally cried for half a day going through the old family movies to create a highlight video for the rehearsal dinner. The movies are priceless.

I've never met parents with grown children who felt they wasted money by taking too many pictures of their kids in the growing-up years.

Cameras don't blink, and these pictures of our family past show the good and the bad, the successes and the failures, the attractive and the not so attractive. That's an important difference between them and the pictures we store in our minds, the memories we keep of our children's past. Those memories can be edited—for free and with computerlike speed—anytime we want to adopt God's forgiveness plan as our attitude toward our kids.

Again the apostle sums it up, this time in his "happy" epistle: "One thing I do: forgetting what lies behind and reaching forward to what lies ahead, I press on toward the goal for the prize of the upward call of God in Christ Jesus" (Phil. 3:13–14).

The recipe for a good marriage always includes the ingredients of two good forgivers and so does the recipe for a good parent-child relationship. I can't recall any teenagers who love and admire their parents who have ever described to me a parent who holds a lot of grudges and reminds them of their past failures. As hard as I try . . . I can't think of even one!

But I have encountered many boys and girls who displayed on the surface a smorgasbord of teen problems and told me about parents who remind them of their faults. Though it always breaks my heart, it no longer surprises me, after I've spent time counseling a confused teenager, to meet his or her parents and hear their judgmental, critical, unforgiving rhetoric about their child.

Which way are you facing?

If it's the wrong way, turn back to your children. If you harbor the memories of their past failures in the family movies of your mind, take a trip to the cutting room tonight as you say your prayers. Wake up tomorrow and enjoy the beginning of a new relationship with children who need it so.

Give your kids the forgiveness God has given you. He never said, "Hey, change and measure up to my standards, and then I'll love you." He simply said, in dying on the cross, "I love you as you are. I've paid for your mistakes—past, present, and future. Now come and be my child. As your loving Daddy, I'll lead you in the right direction."

Just as our heavenly Father cleaned our slates, so should we seek to wipe our children's slates clean every day.

The Layers Beneath
the Teen Crisis

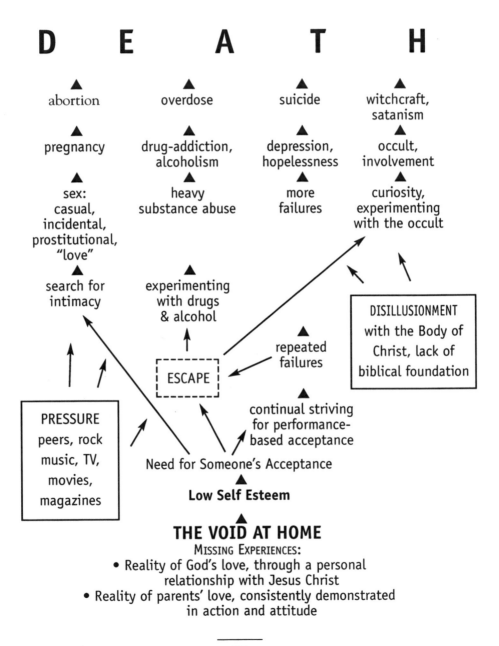

D   E   A   T   H

▲ abortion   ▲ overdose   ▲ suicide   ▲ witchcraft, satanism

▲ pregnancy   ▲ drug-addiction, alcoholism   ▲ depression, hopelessness   ▲ occult, involvement

▲ sex: casual, incidental, prostitutional, "love"   ▲ heavy substance abuse   ▲ more failures   ▲ curiosity, experimenting with the occult

▲ search for intimacy   ▲ experimenting with drugs & alcohol

DISILLUSIONMENT with the Body of Christ, lack of biblical foundation

ESCAPE

▲ repeated failures

PRESSURE
peers, rock music, TV, movies, magazines

▲ continual striving for performance-based acceptance

Need for Someone's Acceptance
▲ **Low Self Esteem**
▲ **THE VOID AT HOME**

MISSING EXPERIENCES:
• Reality of God's love, through a personal relationship with Jesus Christ
• Reality of parents' love, consistently demonstrated in action and attitude

time \tim\ n. 1. Something we're all given equal amounts of each day. 2. What must be invested now—or lost forever.

9

Take Me Fishing Again

As for man, his days are like grass;
As a flower of the field, so he flourishes.
When the wind has passed over it, it is no more;
And its place acknowledges it no longer.
—PSALM 103:15–16

Each day is a lifetime in miniature.

"How much longer is Pardner going to live?"

When little Cooper asked the question that night, the atmosphere inside our car became chilled and silent. My stomach felt hollow.

Pardner never let us call her Grandma—she said she wasn't old enough to be a grandma. (She lived to be one hundred years young.)

She was a born fisherman. She lived on the lake and caught fish when the fishing guides couldn't get a bite. Going fishing with her was always fun . . . and always successful.

Earlier that night, Pardner had called my family over to her house to give my two boys her fishing rods and tackle box. She knew her fishing days were over. My four kids, who so admired their great-grandmom, couldn't understand why.

And I'll never understand why such a wonderful lady had to leave this planet where her kids and grandkids and great-grandkids adored her. But I'm trying to be mature enough to leave the questions alone until the curtain between time and eternity is raised for me.

I wish I could have gone fishing with her more. I wish I could hear again her classic East Texas Bonnie-and-Clyde stories of the depression days she lived through.

I wish I would have shown more gratitude for her tireless efforts to please her kin.

Funny how time slips away.

Funny how we let it go unnoticed.

Funnier still how the only thing on earth that matters on nights like that night is family. In that fragile moment, the created things that surrounded us were empty of value. I couldn't have cared less about Pardner's will.

When the final song is playing, when the remaining grains of sand are so few in a loved one's hourglass of time . . . our life's priorities distill to their purest value. And the certainty hits: You never spend enough time with your family.

How much longer is Pardner going to live? I don't know, little Cooper.

As I said my prayers that night after tucking my foursome into bed, a renewed tenderness flowed through my mind. How much longer will any of them be with us?

Soon, Debbie-Jo and I will have spent almost twenty-five years together in this house. I wish we could spend a hundred. I don't see her as much as I wish I did. We don't hold hands enough. There's so much about her childhood that I've never taken time to learn.

As for Brady, Cooper, Jamie, Courtney . . . it feels like just last Wednesday they were learning how to walk. Then yesterday (it seems), I woke up and found myself well on my way to becoming a grandpa.

Getting enough time with your family is like trying to grab a tug-of-war rope that your opponents are pulling swiftly through your hands. The harder you try, the more it burns.

I can't hold on to it, but I can cherish every minute of the time I have with them. I can savor every delicious Now between Now and Then. Today I can esteem my kids so highly that if I'm still here when one of their names is called on the roll up yonder, I'll be able to smile and know I took every chance to let that son or daughter know, "You mean so very much to me."

One night I chartered a private plane to come home so I could spend all the next day with my family. It was worth every penny.

Another time, I had to turn down a fantastic opportunity to speak to a prestigious group because little Courtney had a gymnastic meet scheduled that day. And business meetings couldn't happen on Saturday mornings, because that's when Brady played soccer.

A friend of mine owned several dozen small franchise businesses that really kept him hopping from city-to-city. He had been quite successful in his endeavors and wanted to pass his business expertise on to his son. When the boy was fourteen, the father called him into his study for a rare father-son meeting. He looked into his boy's eyes expectantly and asked, "What do you want to be when you're out on your own, son?"

"I don't know," the boy replied. "I just know I don't want to be as busy as you are."

The next day, the father called a meeting with his partner and began drawing up the papers to sell all the franchise stores to the local managers. He kept only two employees in his restructured business—but he also kept his family.

One of my favorite people is a father of two who lives in one of our largest cities. As his children began their critical teenage years, he was becoming a successful oil executive at a time when the oil industry was booming. He was being rewarded with responsibility, company ownership, and large financial gain. But even in the summer he left home before daylight to drive to his downtown office and returned after dark to a lonely supper table.

After praying about his priorities, he quit his job, bought a small computer, and began his own business in his home. His business flopped and he lost countless thousands of dollars, but he gained a son, a daughter, and a wife. The love and respect they feel for their family leader today is immeasurable.

I read recently the story of a first-grade girl who asked her mother why her father brought home a briefcase full of papers every evening. Her mother explained, "Daddy has so much to do that he can't finish it all at the office."

"Why don't they just put him in a slower group?" she wondered.

The most haunting scenes to me in Thornton Wilder's classic play *Our Town* come when Emily is told in the graveyard by the angel that she can return to life to relive one day, but only one day. She decides she wants to return for her twelfth birthday. "Don't do it, Emily," the other townspeople in the graveyard tell her, but she decides to anyway. She wants to see Mama and Papa again.

The scene switches, and there she is, twelve years old, on the morning she remembers with such happiness. She comes down the stairs in a party dress, with her curls bouncing. But her mother is so busy making the cake that she can't stop long enough to really look at her. "Mama," Emily says, "Look at me. I'm the birthday girl!"

"Fine, birthday girl," Mama answers. "Sit down and have your breakfast."

Papa comes in, but he's so busy getting off to work that he never looks at her either. Her brother enters, also absorbed in his own endeavors.

Finally Emily calls out from center stage, "Please, somebody, just look at me." Nobody does. Once more she turns to her mother. "Please, Mama?" Again there's no response. Emily turns to the angel and says, "Take me away. I've forgotten what it was like to be human. Nobody looks at anybody. Nobody cares, do they?"

Children spell love T-I-M-E. Without our consistent commitment of time, love can't be communicated.

Is it time to carefully reevaluate your daily schedule and carve out more moments for your kids?

"How much longer is Pardner going to live?"

Pardner, I didn't want to take those fishing rods home that night. Please take me fishing again.

PART III

You're the Best

Catch your children in the act of doing something good . . . and tell them about it.

self-image \self'-im'-ij\ n. 1. The concept of me that I see through your eyes. 2. "Mirror, mirror, on the wall, who's the favorite of us all?"

10

Making Their Day— and More

My dad believes in me.

> — A TEEN, IN AN ACCEPTANCE SPEECH
> AS NEW STUDENT COUNCIL
> PRESIDENT

My parents think I'm stupid.

> —AMY, A SIXTEEN-YEAR-OLD, AFTER A
> SUICIDE ATTEMPT

During this period of self-doubt (ages twelve to fifteen) the
personality is often assaulted and endangered beyond repair.

> —DR. URIE BRONFENBRENNER

W hen my children were small, I was their mirror. That was one of the most sobering thoughts I ever came to grips with. They saw themselves as I saw them. If I was critical of them, they felt unworthy. If I was positive and enthusiastic about them, they felt valuable.

My sensitive wife planted this truth in my mind one day when I was being overly critical of one of my sons. "Honey," she said, "he wants your approval so badly. He's always looking into your eyes to see how well he's doing."

Most parents feel energized with love and enthusiasm by a newborn family member, an excitement that carries us through all the dirty diapers, spilled milk, and sleepless nights. But by the time that boy or girl reaches junior high age, the mistakes caused by inexperience are no longer little toddler messes—they instead can become major family hassles. The child may have picked up so many of Mom and Dad's negative characteristics that a damper falls on the relationship. At that point too many parents lose the desire to be in their child's fan club any longer, and they give up the All-American hopes that motivated them before. But kids, especially kids in today's world, never outgrow the need for regular shots of praise that charge them into the day with hope.

Kids will never stop trying for a father or mother who thinks they're the greatest.

I feel safe in saying my number-one job in raising my children was the challenging task of helping them develop a healthy self-concept.

I've sifted through the complexities of countless teenagers' hearts during their times of intense crisis, and amazingly I've discovered that almost every tragic problem has the same root. The conversation may begin with talk about an abortion, a drug addition, or a rebellious attitude; but after a lot of time and empathy, when the layers of complex emotions are peeled away, almost without fail a low self-image is uncovered.

Kids become so transparent when they realize the lack of direction in their lives. At a youth rally recently, I spoke to kids gathered from several small towns in southern Missouri. As usual, I enjoyed most the individual encounters I had with them after the assembly. The more teenagers I talked with that night, the more I heard about their having nothing to do after dark in these small towns (like most in America) except ride the loop in their parents' cars, go parking, drink beer, and smoke dope. The blatant sin going on among teenagers in these situations is mind boggling.

But one girl I met that night was different. Her standards were high. Her morals were sound. Her faith in Christ was solid. I asked her why she was different, and the next week she wrote me her answer.

I am proud to say I don't drink, smoke, etc., and that I am completely accepted by my peers. Whenever I am offered anything, I firmly reply "No," and they accept it. I've found that some of my friends feel insecure or that they won't be accepted if they don't go along. You really need to feel confident and sure about yourself so that you don't have to go along to be accepted. I credit all confidence I obtain now to my great parents. I don't know where I'd be without them building me up and telling me how much they love me, not for what I do, but for what I am. I am so happy that I don't do anything I don't want to and that I am not only accepted but respected for my views. I hope other teenagers will start respecting and liking themselves more, so that they can be happy with who they are without doing things they don't want to do.

LOVE, MARIA

P.S. Here's a quotation I read today: "Parents need to fill a child's bucket of self-esteem so high that the rest of the world can't poke enough holes in it to drain it dry."

A healthy self-image is a balance of confidence, humility, and security. More than 90 percent of the job of instilling it is assigned to parents. If you haven't started yet, the time to begin is now, no matter what age your children are.

Here are some simple ways to help make it happen:

1. Say "I love you" every day, both in words and actions. (Builds confidence.)
2. Say "You're very valuable to God and to me" every day, both in words and in actions. (Builds confidence.)
3. On a regular basis, offer loads of encouragement, focusing especially on areas of heart and character development rather than physical appearance, athletic ability, and so on. (Builds security.)
4. Memorize Scripture verses together and review and discuss them every day. (Builds confidence and humility.)

5. Go to God in prayer together every day. (Builds confidence and humility.)

6. When you sin, hurt, or offend, ask for both God's forgiveness and the child's. (By example, builds humility.)

7. Consistently and with joy, serve and submit to your spouse, as well as serve your children. (By example, builds humility.)

8. Regularly in both words and actions, communicate your commitment to your spouse, as well as to your children. (Builds security.)

9. When punishment is required, punish the sin but love the child. (Builds security.)

10. By both example and instruction, teach your children to talk positively about themselves and others. (Builds confidence.)

11. Provide your children with continual opportunities for success experiences. (Builds confidence.)

Though these guidelines are simple, they are time consuming. But it takes only a moment to rip apart this fragile aspect of a child's inner being. Here are some common ways parents do it:

1. Being too proud to say "I'm sorry."

2. Being too proud to submit to and serve another.

3. Finding humor in making cutting remarks to a child or using such remarks when correcting or disciplining.

4. Offering encouragement only for such externals as looks, clothing, hair style, and athletic skills.

5. Comparing their own successes with a child's failures.

6. Letting a child "get away" with disobedience or ungratefulness.

7. Laughing at a child's failures.

8. Letting children have their way when their motives are wrong.

9. Punishing too harshly.

10. Making behavior demands of children that are inconsistent with their own example.

To give you a window into adolescent hearts that have suffered from the parental destruction of self-image, here are quotes from a few letters

I've received from teens:

> If I ever have a question, I'm scared to ask it at home. I hate being yelled at. Now if you were in my shoes, wouldn't you hate yourself too? Well, I do. I hate life.—Amy

> I don't like my dad very much. Not once has he really hugged me. Rarely has he told me he loves me. I feel so awful because I can't ever run to my dad and have him make things okay. I can never cry on my dad's shoulder. Not once has he ever said, "Julie, things will be okay." I want so badly to scream and let out all of this hurt. I feel so alone.—Julie

> You told me you were proud of me. Thanks for making my day. No one ever said that to me before. My dad used to tell me I would never amount to anything. It took a long time to get over that.—Andy

> My mom hurts me so bad. She says one of the reasons she doesn't like me is because I'm dumb, and she says I have never been a healthy kid. My grades are six F's and one D. Maybe I am stupid like my mom tells me.—Sharon

An old story is told of a smart-aleck ten-year-old who came to a wise old man and wanted to make him stumble. The boy had a baby bird in his palm.

Into a face highlighted with wisdom's wrinkles and crowned with gray hair, the boy poked his question: "Sir, is this bird in my hand dead or alive? Tell me, if you are so wise."

Assured that the bird was alive, the old sage knew that if he said it was, the insensitive boy would crush it to death in his hand before opening his palm. If he said the bird was dead, the boy would let it fly away in freedom but mock him for his error.

Looking steadily into the boy's cold eyes, the man said softly, "Son, it is as you will it."

So it is with us. In our hands lie the fragile egos of our children and the power to either crush them or let them soar.

A Healthy Self-Image

A child with a healthy self-image is one who . . .
- understands her or his secure position in Christ.
- finds great favor in her or his parents' eyes.
- realizes the importance of obedience, integrity, and honor.
- is given opportunities for success experiences.

If a child lives with criticism, he learns to condemn.
If a child lives with tolerance, he learns to be patient.
If a child lives with security, he learns to have faith.
If a child lives with fairness, he learns justice.
If a child lives with approval, he learns to like himself.

Vision \vi-zhen\ n. 1. A dream (and more) about happily ever after.

11

Help Them Dream, Help Them Build

Anyone can count the seeds in an apple, but only God can count the apples in a seed.

It's not to fear that a child's life ends in early death . . . but that it never really begins.

One morning, after another of my exhausting daily jogs that hurt worse with every added candle on my birthday cake, I plodded up that long, last hill, knowing that in all rights an ambulance and respirator should be at the top to meet me. At the last curve near the top, I passed a large, gushing fountain I built the second year I worked for my father. Beside it was a twenty-foot sugar maple I planted at the same time, now twenty-five years ago. As I beheld the breathtaking yellow and orange leaves, I forgot for an instant how tired I was. My face lifted. A fresh show of adrenaline gushed through my veins and pushed the lactic acid out of my cramping muscles.

My mind raced back to that exciting time when I was a wet-behind-the-ears college graduate. I felt the warmth of fulfillment as I recalled the winter day when I dug the young maple from the woods with a shovel. And I remembered getting up at dawn, day after day, to drive our two-ton truck deep into the hills of Arkansas and load by hand the thousands of sand rocks that would form the fountain's veneer.

My daddy didn't want to spend the $6,000 the fountain cost, though I did. He was the boss, and I was only a rookie in a business he had slaved thirty years to establish. But he let me build the fountain.

I didn't do everything right. During one crisis in the field engineering stage, as we poured concrete and worked like crazy as it set up, Daddy sweated and worked shoulder-to-shoulder with me so I wouldn't fail.

Daddy taught me how to dream. He dreamed with me. And he helped my dreams come true. The fountain and that sugar maple are monuments not to the kid who built and planted them but to the father who encouraged him along the way. Daddy taught me how to have a vision, to create an idea and help that idea mature into full bloom.

Too many kids in America aren't taught that. They feel like failures. That's why they kill themselves with drugs and bullets and alcohol and thoughtless sex.

Most of these kids have at least one "successful" parent—someone who can put together the big deal. Someone who manages the business well and wins approval from the board of directors. Someone who can make the home happen—the meals, the bills, the shopping, the cleaning, the lawn work, the repairs. Someone who excels at certain hobbies. Someone who can buy and wrap presents. When it all succeeds, we feel good inside, strengthened. Our self-image is lifted. But is something—someone—getting overlooked?

A friend of mine came from a home that knew how to make children feel loved. Her parents adopted two children, ages six and seven, whose mother was a prostitute. The children never knew a father. They literally spent their first few years living in a doghouse with a dog. All they could do verbally was grunt, growl, and bark. Their IQs were measured at 37. The diagnosis was hopeless: "Permanent institutional cases. . . . They'll never be normal."

But they began to discover love. Each day they'd hear over and over again the words "I love you." They were overwhelmed with hugs and pats on the back.

On the day they learned to say the word *love*, they ran in and out of their playroom repeating it countless times. Their first spoken sentence was "I love you," addressed to their mommy and daddy.

In a year's time they were able to read and discuss a daily newspaper.

Showcase

My fortieth birthday is one of my fondest memories. At 7 A.M. my kids burst into my room singing "Happy Birthday" in four different keys. The first to reach the bed where I was still half asleep was Cooper, the youngest, wearing his famous smile. "Happy birthday, Daddy!" he blurted out as he dove into my arms and presented me with my first present of the day. The little lump was wrapped in paper that had been half-folded, half-wadded around it. A piece of secondhand ribbon was taped on top, the ends hanging down limply like a girl's pigtails on a hot summer day.

"Thanks, Cooper," I said with as much enthusiasm and sincerity as I could muster. Inside the wrapping paper I found that the present itself was another piece of paper, tightly wadded up.

"Uh, what is it, Little Buddy?"

"It's a hand grenade, Daddy. Do you like it?"

Sensing his search for assurance, I went off like a New Year's celebration. "You bet I do! Best hand grenade I've ever seen! Did you make it all by yourself?"

"Yes sir, all by myself!"

Over the years, I received many such personally made gifts from Cooper, and I made a trophy of each one.

There are times when a parent must thoughtfully and firmly punish a child for the negatives. But ten times more often (at least) are the moments you can praise a child for the masterpieces that express creative talents.

Our refrigerator was always a showcase for school drawings. My office bulletin board had many pictures and love letters from the hands of my children in their moments of inspiration.

Go for the Heismann

After an exciting September college football telecast, the on-the-field announcer found the happy parents of the quarterback who had just led his team to a spectacular upset. The parents fairly consumed the ABC microphone with expressions of pride for their son as they answered the opening how-do-you-feel question.

"Do you think he deserves the Heismann Trophy?" The commentator continued, shouting over the crowd's victory cheers.

"Of course he does," the father answered with a smile that filled my heart with understanding. "My son was made for the Heismann."

That's it, I thought to myself. That's the secret to successful parenting. The Scripture verse says, "Train up a child in the way he should go . . ."

And where should a child go?

Go for the Heismann Trophy. Go for the best.

Not for a perishable gold statue poised for dust-gathering in a glass case . . . not for being the best player in college football . . . but for being the best in life. The best he or she can be.

Do you believe your child was made for this . . . to be the best?

Teens Talk about Encouragement

Today's teens tell how their parents have both succeeded and failed in meeting their needs for encouragement.

Q: *What specific things do your parents do that make you feel good about yourself?*

Back me up in all I do, discuss problems or joys with me, encourage me in all I do, trust me with a lot of things, spend time with me, share their life and love!

My mom and dad will take time out of their schedules to meet my needs or to be with me. They tell me "I love you" a lot, or "You're a great kid" or "I'm proud of you." They are open with me and will talk to me when I ask them to. They trust me with a lot and give me a lot of freedom to do my own things.

What makes me feel the best is that they trust me so much. They give me a lot of mature responsibility, and they trust me with all their hearts. I love them so much for that trust.

They always tell me that they are proud of me—no matter what I do. I've always had a problem with my grades (I'm just not a good student), but Daddy always tells me that grades are important but that communication with people is more important, and I believe that.

I have a very special relationship with both of my parents. I talk to them about everything. Especially my mom. She's my best friend.

They love me.

They make me feel good about myself by praying with me. They encourage me a lot. They tell me that they love me.

They congratulate me even if I fail. They try and lift my spirits.

They tell me what God is doing in their lives, and they ask me for my advice.

Q: *What do your parents do that makes you feel discouraged?*

Hurt each other.

They get mad at each other and take it out on me.

All in all, my parents know that I am a good, responsible kid. I never do big things to get in trouble for, so they pick on little things. Colossians 3:21 says, "Fathers (parents), don't scold your children so much that they become discouraged and quit trying." Which is so often how I feel. I wanted to give up so many times, and if it weren't for my relationship with Jesus Himself it would have been so easy for me to give up. My sister, on the other hand, is a total opposite. She is kind of a rebel and she gets away with anything, which makes me resentful.

They are perfectionists and point out everything I do wrong. Sometimes they push me too much in activities.

They don't remember to also tell me positive things when they are telling me things I need to work on.

Fight! Every morning, afternoon, and night.

As he gets older, my dad doesn't seem to want to listen or to want to talk as much, although he is a great resource to tap into.

I want to give up. I have nothing here. I barely have a mother and father who appreciate me, love me, and say they're proud of me. Nothing matters anymore. I might as well crawl in a corner of the world and die. God doesn't even want me now. I'll probably get used to hell. I've lived in hell for almost twenty years now, so what's an eternity?

Q: What is one positive thing your parents have done that you remember most?

Told me about Jesus.

My parents told me about Jesus and led me to accept him as my Savior.

They spanked me for seeing my brother do something and not admitting it. They told me if I saw something being done against the rules and I was aware of it and didn't do anything, I was guilty too. I'll never forget that wonderful lesson.

The most positive thing is when they sent me to camp. It changed my life so much. It's given me friends, real ones! Of course, it led me to my best friend—Jesus.

Dad drove two hours out of his way to look at a puppy. My mom picked me up from school and took me to lunch and shopping all day.

When I was seven my dad took me on our "date" on Valentine's Day. We went to a concert of our favorite group and I got to stay out late.

My dad promised to take me kite-flying. He accidentally cut his arm and went to the hospital. He still took me kite flying when he got back.

One time my dad and stepmother drove two hours just to watch a basketball game I was cheering at.

Q: *What is one negative thing your parents have done that will be hardest to forget?*

They punished me for something I didn't do.

They don't listen, and I have to totally get their attention. I feel like I'm not even there and that they aren't paying any attention to me. They don't tell me some of their problems just so I won't be worried with them. I would rather help them and know when they feel upset or discouraged, so I can encourage.

Q: *What special things do your parents do to strengthen your relationship with them?*

Go to church and spend Sundays together with the entire family.

Dad takes me out once a year for my birthday to talk about my next year.

Pray for and with me.

They are very gentle as they tell me or ask me things.

When they know they are wrong (hardly ever), they apologize.

Plan their schedules around the kids.

They let me talk to them about the opposite sex.

They understand my weaknesses. They never compare me with my sister! They are so humble.

cheerleader \chir-le-der\ n. 1. The mom or dad who continually gives encouragement from the sidelines. 2. The parent who truly prays without ceasing for each child.

12

A Cheerleader

I can live two months on one good compliment.
—MARK TWAIN

Today she's my wife. Yesterday she was the enthusiastic girl with long, frosted pigtails that bounced as she ran, a cheerleader par excellence.

With three years of cheerleading experience in junior high, four in high school, and four in college, plus her twenty-five-year directorship of a sport's camp, she's certainly earned the right to be counted in the professional ranks.

To her, cheerleading is a sincere expression of excitement for her team. Sometimes—as I watched her racing up and down the sidelines encouraging the SMU athletes or making the call well before the man in black and white did—I wondered if she didn't put on that red and blue skirt and sweater uniform just so she could be the person closest to the action on the field.

Debbie-Jo has always been a cheerleader. And she's still one today.

Now that her megaphone is in storage, her style is that of a quiet, consistent encourager. She applauds, consoles, encourages.

She reminds me so much of what is perhaps the greatest story the greatest teacher ever told. In Mark 4, Jesus tells his disciples about the farmer who cast his seeds to the wind. Some of them fell where there was no soil (they didn't take root), some fell on rocky, shallow soil (where they sprang up quickly but withered away just as fast), some landed among thorny vines (choked out after sprouting), and some fell among good, deep soil (they grew like crazy—and before long produced new seed for generations).

In her commitment as a cheerleader-mom, Debbie-Jo consistently sowed seeds. Sometimes the kids' hearts were hard and the seeds didn't sprout. But she continued sowing. Some days her good deeds and good words may have gone unnoticed, or maybe noticed but not appreciated. She kept the seeds coming. There were days when her teaching was choked out by the misleading secular influences at school, in textbooks, or from the media. Yet she kept sowing the seeds.

Every now and then, the moment was ripe, the soil deep and fertile with humility. Jamie broke her wrist in volleyball. Courtney tore ligaments in her ankle in gymnastics. Brady sat on the bench in soccer. The teachable moment was upon her. The seeds fell into open hearts.

Debbie-Jo's seeds were always in the air. "Good job, Jamie!" "Brady, I'm proud of you." "Cooper, that was really a super paper you turned in!" "Courtney, I never did it that well when I was growing up!"

A hug, a pat on the back, a tear wiped lovingly from a sad face . . . seeds.

Walking her kids all the way to the bus stop.

Regularly planned special nights out for each child, one-on-one with Mom.

Personal evening Bible studies with the girls.

Attending every school program and athletic event that the kids were in (making for a full calendar, with four children).

Going to the game even when her child was injured and sitting on the bench.

Making lunches every day.

Helping to clean up the mess while encouraging the embarrassed child who made it.

Planning and celebrating a special birthday party with a customized cake and decorations every year for every child.

Creatively giving a special touch to every Christmas, Valentine's Day, Easter, and Thanksgiving.

Always being available to help with homework.

Letting her kids see her unfailing encouragement and support for her husband.

Seeds.

Some end up in the rocks or in the weeds. But any good cheerleader-mom knows that the more seeds she sows, the more seeds will find the perfect, fertile soil and grow.

Now that this cheerleader is about to become a grandmother, I predict that her four kids will spread seeds in the same lavish way . . . and Debbie-Jo's harvest will be multiplied.

I met another cheerleader-mom one summer. With her was her seventeen-year-old son. "Joe," she said, "this is my wonderful son. He's tall because his heart is so big it just keeps pushing him higher and higher." The boy's sense of security and acceptance shined right through his mask of embarrassment.

You don't have to carry pompoms or a megaphone to be a cheerleader. One of my close friends had an alcoholic father who left home early in Keith's life. But Keith had a star for a mom, and he's turned out to be one of the finest Christian men I know.

A talented athlete, Keith recently told me about the greatest event in his sports career. It was Dad's Night at his high school, in his senior year. All the fathers were lined up on the sidelines with their sons' numbers fastened to their shirts. Keith felt alone and depressed as the special observance got underway.

Then suddenly he noticed someone standing in the line wearing his number. His heart skipped a beat: Had Dad come home? Looking closer, a tear entered his eye. There stood his mom, stately as any dad in the line, her hair tucked under her work hat, jeans pressed neatly, and number 24 displayed proudly on her shirt.

Cheerleading is for everyone in the family—which is good, because it's highly contagious.

Any parent who's had to travel for a living knows the excitement and anticipation you feel that last day on the road, when you press through the night on a late flight or late drive to see your much-missed loved ones. After one long, winter road trip, I came home at 2 A.M. to a house covered with "Welcome Home, Daddy!" posters, banners, cards, pictures, and poems. With a lump in my throat, I tiptoed through the confetti and back to my room. I opened my closet to find no less than thirty more signs. All four little ones had gotten into the homecoming preparation. The handwriting (some legible, some only scribbles) spelled out "We missed you!" "We love you!" "We're glad you're back!"

I noticed especially a simple message in runny watercolors. It said in my daughter's eight-year-old honesty, "This is a very good home."

In our very good home we had (as every home has) our struggles, our tears, our unkind words. But we were (and still are) each other's biggest fans. We believe in each other and verbalize that enthusiasm every chance we get.

Perseverance Reaps Rewards

One of the most respected heroines in our nation's history has a fascinating but little-known life story.

In a basement cell of an old New England psychiatric home late in the last century, an unresponsive, cataleptic, schizophrenic patient lay curled in a ball on a bench. She had been written off as incurable. She spoke not a word and would not move from her fetal position.

A housemaid passed her cell each day on her rounds. She would shove a plate of food under the door to the "hopeless" girl inside. Before leaving, she also would gently nudge the girl with the end of her mop handle. As she communicated with the girl day after day with the only means she had, she was saying, "Someone out here cares for you. You haven't been forgotten."

As the weeks and months went by, the girl began to come out of her ball. She began to receive the food with her hands. Soon she was sitting up. As time went by, she began to communicate with the housekeeper and eventually was totally cured.

Later the director of the home was confronted by a desperate man from Tuscumbia, Alabama. He requested someone who could work with a blind, deaf mute, a girl who also had received the "hopeless" label. The director introduced the man to the miraculously cured girl who had occupied the basement cell—Annie Sullivan—and thus began her historic work with Helen Keller.

Love meets practical needs any way it can—even if all you have to work with is a mop handle! Although our children's attitudes and actions may sometimes be so disappointing as to make the situation seem hopeless, parents who continue to serve such children will be rewarded.

coach \koch\ *n.* 1. Not a referee or an umpire, but a teacher who brings out the best in another. 2. If you love me, you can know me; if you know me, you can show me.

13

A Coach

A boy is the only thing God can use to make a man.
—CAL FARLEY

After winning the national collegiate basketball championship a few years ago, the smiling coach was given the ABC microphone with the question, "Aren't you proud of yourself now? Isn't this great for your career?"

"Nah, that's not what makes it great." The coach reached back into the crowd pressing around him to bring before the camera one of his jubilant players. "This is what it's all about," he said.

Great coaches don't work for titles and trophies. Their aim is to develop their players. Legendary football coach Bear Bryant expressed this philosophy in working with his players: "When something goes bad, I did it. When something goes not so good, we did it. When something goes great, they did it."

I played under several coaches during my eleven years of football. Though some won more games than others, each season came and went just the same, and each coach got the basic job done. But the coaching styles were definitely an assortment.

I still bristle at the memory of one man whose motivational method was to kick his players fiercely in the rear after they bent into their stance for the next play. That was torture.

The two best coaches I had the opportunity of playing for were Ray Utley and Hayden Fry. Polar opposites in personality, both had unique styles that still help me as a dad.

Both men knew their players—not their weight, their speed, or their latest bench press, but their hearts. They knew that not all players are motivated the same way. Some of us needed extra wind sprints. Some needed time after practice to talk. Others needed a raised voice or a half game on the bench. Our team was small and under-talented, but we went to the games united and motivated because those two men cared.

By knowing each player's individual bent and by investing energy to bring out the best in that player, the great coach finds significance.

Great fathers do the same thing.

One such father I know in Texas had a struggling seventeen-year-old son. He let him design and build his own house, a project that took two years to complete. With his father as "coach," the boy laid every log, drove every nail, poured every footing, and tacked on every shingle. When the fantastic experience was over, so were the teenage years . . . and two friends walked away, proudly.

Another dad found his father-son niche in race cars. He and his son bought twin cars and traveled the nation racing together. In one recent race, the son took the cup after unintentionally forcing out his dad. But the dad walked away the bigger champion.

In the process of building a business empire, another father felt he was losing his son. After we talked, he decided to take off his business suit at night and put on mechanic's clothes to help his son work on his Volkswagen. He's finding his son again.

My own dad towed a Model A Ford six hundred miles so my brother could have a success experience rebuilding that antique under Daddy's guidance.

Coaches seldom go out on the playing field during game time. For a father, too, there comes a time to stay on the sidelines while his child goes alone into the arena to face the game of life. Our influence now depends solely on the job we did before the game—teaching, training, encouraging, preparing our son or daughter for this moment.

That takes faith.

It happened every time my daughter went on a date or my son caught the bus to go to school. They went without their cheerleader-mom and without their father-coach.

It kept us on our knees—a good place for a cheerleader and coach to be.

The key to winning these games is to practice hard and pray heartily. My daddy always reminded me to work like it all depends on me and pray like it all depends on God. "Between the two of you," he said, "you'll come out a winner."

The practice field is yours and mine—the place to stay close to our children, to direct and nurture them. Good practice makes good games.

But the playing field belongs to our kids and to God. During the game is the time for trust. It's the time for growth, the growth that is a mystery known only to God. To him we pray. To him goes the glory for the victories we'll see.

Great Coaches

Bear Bryant

"He cared for his players."

by Gene Stallings

It was midnight. On the following day we were to play Baylor University. Texas A&M was in the midst of Bear Bryant's worst season (one win, nine losses) in his thirty-eight years of coaching. He came into the football dormitory and called the entire team into the lobby. He opened his Bible, and in his customary down-to-earth manner, retold the parable of the mustard seed.

I'll never forget the concern for us, as people, that he communicated that night. He felt the hurt and embarrassment we and our families were feeling. He told us we didn't have much in the eyes of the public, but that we were winners if we didn't give up. He helped us believe we'd win in a bigger game—the game of life.

Three years later, we won the Southwest Conference Championship and for a while were number one in the nation.

Bear Bryant, who went on to become the winningest coach in football history, was unsurpassed in his profession because he cared for his players. Only those of us who had the privilege of playing for "The Bear" really know how much he cared. He was tough and intense, but he loved us from his heart. The love we felt from him translated into victory after victory, because love brings out the best in people.

Most coaches get the maximum out of some players, but Coach Bryant got the maximum out of all of them. You didn't want to disappoint this man who cared for you.

It didn't take a superstar to win his care. If you were Joe Namath you felt it, and if you barely made the team you felt it. He'd handle you gently when you made a bad play. He never criticized a player publicly. And if you had a special need, you could depend on Coach Bryant to help you out.

He always told us never to get too big or too busy to go to church on Sunday or to take time to write our moms and dads. I loved him for the man he was, for what he stood for, and for what he did for people.

After playing under him and being on his coaching staff, I took the reins at Texas A&M, where he had been my coach a decade before. Ironically, we won the Southwest Conference Championship and met my teacher and his Alabama team in the Cotton Bowl. On that unforgettable day, A&M beat Alabama. After the game, instead of customarily shaking my hand, Coach Bryant picked me up to carry me off the field. Later he came over to our locker room. I excused myself from reporters to meet him at the door. He said candidly, "I didn't come to see you; I came to congratulate your players. They outplayed mine, and I want to tell them how much I respect them for it."

Bear Bryant once told the sports world that he retired from coaching because he felt the players deserved better than he was giving them. No one agreed. There'd never been any better.

John Wooden

"Never departing from the fundamentals"

by Ralph Drollinger

I had just arrived as a freshman at UCLA to play under John Wooden, the most successful college basketball coach in history. We were fifteen former high school All-Americans, later to become the season's national champions.

And here we were on the first day of practice . . . learning how to properly put on our socks and shoes. *Didn't I learn this in first grade?* I thought.

Lesson one was with the socks. Under his close scrutiny, Coach Wooden had us carefully roll them up, like you would your shirt-sleeves. Next we laboriously unrolled them up and over our feet toward the calf muscle. Like Sherlock Holmes with a magnifying glass, he paced the room during the process looking for a tiny, sinful wrinkle in the rows of thirty oversized white feet. He had us run our hands several times over the cotton surface to make sure we'd executed the fundamentals correctly.

The next lesson was on lacing up our shoes. "You mustn't pull the top laces until you put tension in the bottom laces," he said with obvious years of experience. I didn't question his sanity. Echoes of success permeated the place, casting me in a spell of reverential belief that this was the right thing to be doing the first day of practice.

After graduating from UCLA, having performed the same fundamental procedure for years in professional competition, I found myself still executing it carefully. My uneducated teammates smarted at me as I patiently applied my footwear, but that didn't bug me. I knew from experience that more smarting would soon occur after practice—on their feet.

Coach Wooden's philosophy stressed the proper execution of the fundamentals, which were learned by a daily repetition. His approach to a seemingly complex game was simple and basic, never departing from the fundamentals.

Since you couldn't perform these basic maneuvers with blistered feet, the wise coach began his session lecturing on socks and shoes. After dressing our feet, we would do drills without the ball so our concentration centered on executing the physical motion correctly rather than on the results. This helped form good habits, which are difficult to learn if you're temporarily having good results with poor habits.

We who desire to be excellent Christian parents and leaders can learn a main ingredient of success from one of sport history's greatest coaches—a man who so vividly exemplified the scriptural principle of repeating continually the grass-roots basics. Day after day, we must properly put on our socks and shoes . . . to "run the race so as to win the prize."

Tom Landry

"Creative Genius"

by Walt Garrison

When I came to Dallas in 1966, we were far from being the NFL's best team. We were all firmly convinced that very soon we would be. We were playing for the best coach in the game . . . the creative genius of the National Football League.

A creative coach lets you know where you're going and the steps it will take to get there. I learned how the game all fit together from Tom Landry. He taught us how to combine discipline, knowledge, conditioning, motivation, goal setting, confidence, and control to build a winning team.

He believed we had the information to beat anyone. So I studied harder at Dallas than I ever did in college. He taught us that if we were better prepared, we'd win. Football is a game of the split-second edge, and the team that has it will beat its opponent. With our trips, divides, motions, sings, and preshifts we could confuse the defense for a fraction of a second and get that edge. We began to win. Soon we were in the Super Bowl.

He has a creative way of handling people too. When you got stomped, he'd find something good you did to comment on and build you up. When you did great and felt pretty confident, he'd bring you down to earth.

Against Philadelphia one Sunday, I pulled in an easy pass with one hand. During the film session on Monday, everyone laughed and made remarks like, "Way to make it look easy." When they quieted down I heard Coach Landry say softly, "Don't ever drop one." I got the message.

During the first half of the 1970 Super Bowl, I got beat up all over. I was broken and bruised worse than I had ever been. On the bench the trainer was working with my injuries. Coach Landry walked by and spoke to the trainer: "Can he play?"

"I don't know," was the reply.

"I hope so," Landry said. "We need him."

I was back after half time and caught a touchdown pass to help us win. I would have played if my leg was cut off. Just to hear him say that word of encouragement was like a trumpet blast.

When you have faith in a man, you'll run through brick walls for him.

The things Coach Landry taught me mean more to me today than they did when I played for him. I've found that the same things that win on the football field also bring victory in the family and in life as well.

personality \per-sun-al-i-te\ n. 1. The part of your child you love the most 2. The part of your child that drives you crazy.

14

Strengths and Weaknesses

I had a serious problem during my wife's second pregnancy. My first little girl (who turned out to be virtually a clone of her mom) had so won my heart that I didn't think I could ever love another child as I did her.

The birth of number two easily remedied the problem!

I found it easy to love both girls equally. But I also learned that it takes a whole different part of me to love each one. The only thing they seem to have in common is a last name.

In fact, I even seriously questioned whether second daughter Courtney had the same parents as first daughter Jamie. Genetics sure deals some interesting hands! Jamie the brunette is reserved, thoughtful, consistent, even-tempered. Courtney the blond is outgoing, straightforward, spontaneous, excitable.

Fortunately, both have absorbed their mom's character qualities that keep me immersed in a sea of admiration and respect.

The two boys who followed them continued the neat trick of pulling totally unique personalities from the same set of parental genes. Our third child, Brady, is sensitive, aesthetic, self-disciplined, conscientious, analytical. Cooper, fourth in line, is friendly, talkative, enthusiastic, carefree, generous.

Every time I went into a different kid's room, I had to change hats.

If I had disciplined Cooper the same way I disciplined Jamie, he'd think he was a total failure and might never recover. One good stern look would take care of Cooper for a month.

Jamie cried over an injured goldfish but never shed a tear during a spanking. Courtney cried at the first mention of discipline but might just as quickly push a dog aside as pet him.

Courtney wrote great "I'm sorry" notes after she'd been corrected. Jamie kept her cool.

I thoroughly enjoyed the process of studying and understanding the strengths and weaknesses of our kids . . . and seeing how uniquely and wonderfully each one has been gifted. It's an adventure every parent can have.

But first, here's a list of what not to do as you go along:

1. Never compare a daughter's weakness to her mother's strength.
2. Never compare a son's weakness to his father's strength.
3. Never compare one sibling's weakness to another one's strength.
4. Don't insist on or expect the same response from any two children in the same situation.
5. Never focus on the negative side of a child's personality.
6. Never fail to notice the evidence of a child's strengths; instead, take every opportunity to build them up even more.
7. Never stop learning more. Aim continually to really know your child.

Our children's personalities are wonderfully created—uniquely programmed by God. One result is that each child's shortcomings cause him or her to need and depend on siblings and parents in order to reach his or her full potential. It's a process of mutual enabling and strengthening . . . and it's good!

Another result is that each child's list of strengths has a corresponding set of weaknesses. And that's good too.

Why?

The fine art of successful parenting involves focusing on and building up the strengths of each child, and thereby overcoming the weaknesses. But if you're like me (and like 99 percent of all parents), your tendency much of the time will be to focus on the weaknesses. If we do, the result in the child's life may well be low self-esteem, a sense of acceptance based only on performance, moodiness and depression, susceptibility to peer pressure, and a greater likelihood of drug and alcohol use and premarital sex.

Rather than focusing on a child's evident weaknesses, which we tend to see clearly, you can instead use these as clues to understand that child's strengths.

My good friend Wes Neal has studied in-depth this area of strengths and corresponding weaknesses. In the following chart, I pass along his observations to stimulate your thoughts in this area.

When a weakness in your child surfaces, look for the strength that's like a Siamese twin of that weakness. Discipline yourself not to focus on the weakness but instead to search for the strength—like a gold nugget in a pile of ore. Do this consistently, and you'll be well on your way to helping your child perfect and refine the treasure in his or her personality.

Strengths and Related Weaknesses

Analytical ....Critical
Appreciative ....Insincere
Assertive ....Domineering
Communicative ....Overtalkative
Concerned ....Worrying
Confident...........................Self-sufficient
Counseling.........................."Know-it-all"
Courageous ....Reckless
Curious...............................Nosey
Determined ....Stubborn
Diplomatic ....Weak-willed
Effective ....Rigid
Encouraging ....Flattering
Expressive ....Flowery
Forgiving ....Overlenient
Generous ....Wasteful
Imaginative ....Day-dreaming
Listening ....Noncommunicative
Loyal ....Idolizing
Moral ....Judgmental
Obedient ....Overdependent
Open-minded.....................Indecisive
Optimistic ....Unrealistic
Orderly...............................Perfectionistic
Sensitive ....Oversensitive
Spontaneous ....Undisciplined
Stable ....Dull
Straightforward ....Harsh
Thrifty ....Stingy
Tolerant ....Fainthearted

Do your kids a favor today: Complete the following chart (or use a sheet of paper with three columns marked off). In the first two columns, under the headings "Strengths" and "Corresponding Weaknesses," make a list of each child's evident character qualities, both positive and negative. Put corresponding strengths and weaknesses on the same line. Remember, your focus is to be on each child's positive qualities. If weaknesses come to mind more readily, use these simply as clues to uncover the matching strengths.

In the third column, under the heading "My Goals," list ideas on how you can constructively build up each strength . . . and overcome the corresponding weakness without damaging the child's self-image.

STRENGTHS	CORRESPONDING WEAKNESSES	MY GOALS

grace \gras\ n. 1. Love and protection freely bestowed. 2. No strings attached. 3. Christmas and your birthday, every day of the year.

15

Fifty Phrases to Encourage Your Child

(For Everyday Use)

1. You're so much fun to be around!
2. You get better at that every time I see you. Way to go!
3. Hang on a second while I call *Sports Illustrated*—they'll want a picture of this!
4. I'm going to brag about this. That's great!
5. I look up to you!
6. That's the best _____ I've ever seen!
7. You are so thoughtful!
8. This is a tremendous improvement!
9. Good for you!
10. You're such a joy to us!
11. I never did that well when I was your age!
12. Can I put this on the bulletin board at the office so I can see it every day?

13. You handled that beautifully!
14. That's incredible!
15. You're always teaching me something wonderful!
16. They just didn't make kids as good as you when I was growing up!
17. You're really special to me—and getting more special every day!
18. Keep that up and you'll be the world champion someday!
19. I really enjoy being with you!
20. What a super effort!
21. The guy or girl who marries you will be so lucky!
22. That's worth a trophy ten feet high!
23. Your mom and I are so grateful to be your parents!
24. I need to get word to the White House about this—the president will want to know about it!
25. I really enjoy your smile!
26. That's fabulous!
27. There you go! That's it!
28. You're so helpful! Thank you!
29. You're going to make it!
30. God is truly a miracle worker—to produce a kid as great as you from ordinary parents like us!
31. I wish I could have done it that well!
32. You'll always be in my hall of fame!
33. I'm impressed!
34. I know you worked very hard on that. Wonderful job!
35. You're the best!
36. You sure know how to do it right! Outstanding!
37. I love to hear your laugh!
38. You're something else!
39. That's amazing! How did you do that?
40. You take my breath away!
41. You never cease to amaze me!
42. I really like that!
43. Sensational!

44. Absolutely superb!
45. I believe in you!
46. Excellent! That's the way to do it!
47. You make my day!
48. Fantastic!
49. You make me so happy!
50. I love you!

PART IV

Safe at Home

What you value, your child will value.

example \ig-zam-pel\ n. 1. The kind of life that keeps prompting the comment, "When I grow up, I want to be like you"; a model worthy of imitation. 2. "Do as I do."

16

Oh, Those X-Ray Eyes!

Dear Miss Ellerby: When I grow up,
I want to do exactly what you do. Please do it better.

—LETTER FROM A CHILD TO TELEVISION
NEWS COMMENTATOR LINDA ELLERBY

Your greatest opportunity, bar none, to teach your kids the character qualities you want to see in their lives is in how you live your daily life. They watch every move you make, hear every tone of your voice, and seem to be especially keen at picking up actions and attitudes that contradict your verbal messages.

I believe this is the most sensitive area of effective leadership in the home. It's also the kind of parenting that carries the highest price tag. It will probably cost you a lot in terms of giving up pride, relinquishing certain habits, shaping up many neglected areas of your personal life, and learning how to change and adapt.

There is so much at stake in a child's tender years. How can we gamble with that child's perceptions and values by maintaining areas of questionable behavior in our lives?

Children do give their parents room for failure—but in general they cling to what they see in their parents everyday lives. Parents who try to hide certain personal habits from a child—or who try to rationalize actions that are even remotely inconsistent with the lifestyle they want their children to live by—are tiptoeing on thin ice, and at the very least will cause inconsistencies in their children's behavior.

Our kids have x-ray eyes when it comes to seeing our inconsistencies. Congruence, that old mathematical term from geometry class, comes back to haunt me. Even now, I examine my habits daily to see if they match what I want to see in my kids' lives. My lifestyle must set the pace for how I want my children to live.

More than anything else, I want them to see a father whose number-one goal in life is to love God with all his heart. I want them to see in me the ability to ask for forgiveness and to get back up after I've fallen on my face in failure (which I seem to do regularly). I want them to see that integrity is more important than making a dime or a dollar. I want them to see me treating my body with purity, diligently training it for the awesome responsibility of being a temple of the Holy Spirit.

Finally, I want them to see how their very average dad loves their very priceless mother with uncompromising dedication . . . and that he would walk around this planet to convince his children how precious each one of them is.

No Price Tag

A successful parent's example can't be bought . . . at any price.

The story is told of a desperate businessman who propositioned his receptionist with an offer for an extramarital affair. When rebuffed, he added one thousand dollars to make the offer more attractive—knowing that she and her husband were undergoing financial difficulty. Reluctantly, she accepted.

Then he lowered his bid to one hundred dollars.

"A hundred dollars!" she exclaimed. "What kind of a woman do you think I am?"

"You've already shown me what kind of woman you are," he returned. "Now I just want to know your price."

If there's a price tag on the principles I want to live by . . . the principles I want my children to gain from our home . . . then eventually, someone will name it and I'll fall.

If we're not willing to keep those principles so priceless that we always live out those qualities, then our teaching to our children is in vain.

Example is to training a child what railroad tracks are to a freight train or wings to an airplane. Knowing that a child's eyes are always watching, an effective parent will not sell out his or her life principles at any price.

As I counsel America's hurting teenagers, I so often find that their bad habits and major failures were learned from the example of their mom and dad. The carpet into my office has a worn pathway from teenagers who tell the same tragic story . . .

Sixteen-year-old, brown-eyed Mary had an abortion.

Her mom has a boyfriend.

Eighteen-year-old Andy went to jail with two DWI's.

His daddy caps every evening with martinis.

Martin has a hard time telling the truth.

His dad evades the IRS with falsified financial reports.

Sally is a strong-willed, rebellious sixteen-year-old.

Sally's mom is the family dictator.

Bill lost his driver's license over speeding tickets.

Bill's parents use radar detectors in their cars.

Amy and Greg wage a constant sibling rivalry.

Their dad is snappy and quick-tempered with both of them.

Julie is the most unpopular kid at school because she hits anyone who gets in her way.

Her body bears the marks of hasty backhands from her demanding mother.

It would be naive to say that every problem a teenager experiences is a direct result of an inconsistency in a parent's life. Some of the finest parents I know today are having great problems with their teenagers.

But most child psychologists agree that children often become aggravated, rebellious, and irresponsible when they misunderstand and imitate the behavior they see in their parents.

The Greatest Debt

The greatest part of my extensive indebtedness to my parents is for how I saw them live their lives.

I've had time to forget my dad's faults and mistakes during our growing-up years, and I'm sure he had his share. But I'm firmly convinced that he made (and continues to make) many sacrifices to be a man who walks his talk. I can't tell you how much I respect him because of it!

Frankly, I can't tell you anything he ever told me about loving a wife, but I'll never forget seeing the love notes he often left my mom when he left our house early for work. Nor will I forget the respect and tenderness he always showed her.

Daddy's knees must be callused from his consistent evening quiet time before the Lord. He didn't need to talk with us about the importance of prayer. He earned the right to demand purity of speech in our lives because I never heard him utter a four-letter word.

I don't remember Mom telling us how happy we'd be as parents someday if we learned the joy of serving our spouses and children, but I cherish the memories of watching her gather and wash our dirty clothes, scrub our dirty dishes, and with a soft smile carefully pack our lunches for school. The wrinkles on her precious face are the trophies of the pleasure she learned to derive as she served my daddy and her three often ungrateful sons day after day.

Oscar Daddy

When our children were small, every spring I encouraged my wife to go on a week's vacation with her girlfriends. With four children, a husband, a demanding job, and a house to keep, she needed it! My number-one priority in setting an example as a father was to show my appreciation and admiration for the one in our home who served as psychologist, sociologist, director of purchasing, financial planner, household executive, referee, maitre d', sanitation supervisor, counselor-in-chief, and expert in pediatrics, community relations, religion, economics, entertainment, and horticulture—my wife! Another reason for having her leave for a while was so I could understand and appreciate even better all that she did each day.

One such spring, after "batching it" for six days, I awoke with lingering tiredness on a beautiful Easter morning. For this special day, I had been left with a new roll of film and brand-new, hand-sewn Easter clothes for our growing foursome.

Being a clutz around the house, it was all I could do to get all four little bodies bathed and dried while getting breakfast cooked, Sesame Street place mats laid (featuring separately Burt, Ernie, Big Bird, the Cookie Monster, and Oscar the Grouch), and the table set. Then I had to get Easter clothes secured right-side-out for Mommy's welcome-home picture. My nerves were frazzled.

The straw that broke the camel's back was the white tights that somehow had to go over the plump little legs and bottoms of my two daughters. Those tights might have fit a Barbie doll, but certainly the manufacturer didn't have a fumble-fingered bachelor in mind when the nylon was measured for this unreasonable task of dressing up two growing girls. I tried and tried to make them stretch to their waists. Wrinkled ankles and baggy crotch was the best I could do.

Finally, we sat down to lukewarm oatmeal amid accusations that "paste" was a better description of my concoction. While reaching out to join hands in prayer, I knocked a place mat to the floor. It happened to be Oscar the Grouch. I went on with the prayer, saying hurriedly, "Dear Lord, thank you for Easter and the joy of this day. And thank you for the food. Amen."

As I leaned down to pick up the place mat, a small voice whispered in the air, "You better have Oscar today, Dad."

"What did you say?" I snapped at our oldest, whose smirk gave away the source.

"I just thought you might want to keep the Oscar place mat today," she said.

I had heard her correctly the first time. "What did you mean by that remark?" I demanded.

She cleared her throat courageously. "Well, you prayed about the joy of Easter, but it's sort of hard to believe because you're kind of a grouch this morning."

We all got tickled and laughed together at Oscar Daddy. But she was right, and the truth penetrated through the humor. I made a fresh determination to work—and I mean work—on setting a better example. Boy, did I fail! And usually the letdowns don't end with laughter, as at my Oscar Easter breakfast. But the results have been well worth the sweat.

memorizing \mim-or-iz-ing\ v. 1. The activity of feeding your mind. 2. A sure-fire way to replace the negative images of the media with the truths of God's Word.

17

That's Not in There, God!

Thy word I have treasured in my heart,
that I may not sin against Thee.
—PSALM 119:11

I was in a cafe in Nashville, calling home to Southern Missouri after two weeks of lonesome business travel. Debbie-Jo told me she had just finished her prized traditional evening time of tucking the children into bed with prayers. As she had said good night to our two boys in their superhero pajamas, Super Cooper said he wanted to memorize a new Bible verse so he could tell it to his daddy when he came home. "Get out my Bible," he said in his four-year-old dialect, "and wead me one, okay?"

"Cooper," she replied, "the lights are out—can I just tell you one?"

"Okay."

She pulled out the old standby. "A good verse for every child to know is: 'Children, obey your parents, for this is pleasing to God.' "

There was a long pause. Finally Cooper spoke. "That's not in there, Mommy."

"Yes it is, sweetheart."

"No," he protested, "I think you just made that one up."

I roared with laughter as Debbie-Jo gave the account over the telephone. After I hung up and walked back to my table, the truth struck my heart like a sword. That's exactly what I tell God when I keep a safe distance from a Bible verse that demands not only my attention but also my action—especially when he asks me to change something I don't want to change.

That's not in there, God!

Oh, yes it is! All of it is in there, and it's all from our infinitely wise parent in heaven who cared enough to communicate his truths in a love letter written literally with his blood.

The passage that day that pressed me onward into action, sacrifice, planning, and time management was Deuteronomy 6:5–9.

> And you shall love the Lord your God with all your heart and with all your soul and with all your might. And these words, which I am commanding you today, shall be on your heart; and you shall teach them diligently to your sons and shall talk of them when you sit in your house and when you walk by the way and when you lie down and when you rise up. And you shall bind them as a sign on your hand and they shall be as frontals on your forehead. And you shall write them on the doorposts of your house and on your gates.

If I could place in your palm a three-hundred-page book that would absolutely guarantee you a successful multimillion-dollar business, would you read it? Would you memorize key statements in it? Would you think about it continually as you went about your business day by day and week by week? Undoubtedly you would.

I can't promise you that kind of business experience, but God's book promises you many times more than a multimillion-dollar value. It promises you a successful future for your children if you teach them his word day after day, if you memorize it together night after night, and apply it in your home in every situation. Yet of all the kids I've surveyed on this, only 8 percent have parents who take God at his word and memorize Scripture together consistently as a family.

An Inside Look

A friend of mine named Jack Herschend built from scratch one of the country's most creative theme parks and named it Silver Dollar City. It began humbly enough with a small general store atop a large, beautiful crystal cave in Branson, Missouri. In the forty years since then, Jack has put every available penny into his dream of expanding the enterprise into a park that would literally bring back to life the Ozarks of the 1880s.

Today, Silver Dollar City is a multimillion-dollar mix of clever attractions, rides, and craft displays, all in a hillbilly atmosphere. But the feature that gets the most attention by far for the money it cost to create is a silver-dollar-sized hole in an out-of-the-way fence. The hole is just about eye level to a twelve-year-old boy. A small sign above the hole reads, "Don't Look in This Hole." Needless to say, no one passes by without a peek. Behind the hole is a ridiculous picture that makes you wonder why you bothered looking.

In the midst of all the media messages that constantly contend for your family's attention, I'd like to erect a simple fence with a peephole at your eye level, with a "Don't Look" sign to work the same magic it does on the fence in Silver Dollar City.

Step up to the old weathered wood, wink your left eye, and put your right squarely against the peephole. What you'll see could be the most compelling picture your parenting eyes will ever behold.

You recognize immediately the prominent figure in the foreground: He is tall, lean, dark, bearded; his thin, granite face is highlighted by heavy eyebrows set above eyes that are deep and penetrating, seemingly with power both to stare into your heart and to grace it with compassion.

With a voice as powerful as his gaze, Lincoln speaks. His words, well over a century old, are like the brush strokes of a skilled master, painting an alarming portrait of prophetic wisdom for today:

> We have grown in numbers, wealth, and power as no other nation has grown, but we have forgotten God. We have forgotten the gracious hand that preserved us in peace and multiplied and enriched and strengthened us. We have vainly

imagined that all of these blessings were produced by some superior virtue and wisdom of our own. . . . Intoxicated with unbroken success, we have become too self-sufficient to feel the necessity of redeeming and preserving grace, too proud to pray to the God that made us.

The painter's brush is passed from Honest Abe to the even greater hands of the God Lincoln worshiped, and these words are added to the masterpiece, echoing the first psalm:

> How blessed is the man [every father and mother, every
>   boy and girl] . . .
> [Whose] delight is in the law of the Lord,
> And in His law he meditates day and night.
> And he will be like a tree firmly planted by streams of
>   water,
> Which yields its fruit in its season,
> And its leaf does not wither;
> And in whatever he does, he prospers.

Press your eye even closer and look intently: In the background, a choir of saintly fathers and mothers from ages past completes the picture. As you scan first one face and then another and another, each figure speaks with earnest, pleading counsel: "The greatest thing you can do for your children is to pitch a tent in their minds where the treasure chest of God's Word can dwell."

When you're sure the entire scene is fixed firmly in your mind, turn around to examine your own home. Does the heartbeat of Scripture sound in every life?

Our kids need to memorize the first psalm and learn how essential it is not to walk in the counsel of the wicked but instead to meditate on God's Word day and night. Their computers must be programmed with the cleansing power of the knowledge of God's will in their lives.

As parents we must teach them Psalm 23, whose words will convey to their hearts the security and peace of knowing the Lord as their Shepherd.

They need to learn Philippians 2 and then together experience the deepened joy of a family that practices the Christlike unselfishness of loving each other sacrificially.

Together with our children, we must memorize Matthew 5 and become completely convinced that true happiness depends on trusting Christ.

From memorizing portions of John's gospel, we and our children must see the divine characteristics of Jesus and give back to him our praise and worship.

The Magic

I'll never forget the moment when my inadequacy for the task of fatherhood first dawned on me. Our firstborn daughter was sleeping tenderly in her crib at age six months. As I watched her, I was suddenly overcome with a sense of responsibility, love, and humility. "God!" I prayed, "I can't handle this alone. No way can I be this little doll's ultimate authority. I need you to take over the job."

Slowly—but consistently—I began to memorize Scripture. Once her third birthday had passed, I began passing on to her what I had memorized, verse by verse. She's now caught up with me, because her brain works at 78 rpm and mine plays at $33^1/_3$.

As we continue memorizing, the magic comes especially in two different ways.

First, by reinforcing the fact that God and his Word are her authorities in life, it gives her "temporary daddy" the freedom to fail and a basis for recognizing and being forgiven for that failure. An early example came when she was still three, and I swatted her on the bottom in a moment of anger. I knew it was wrong when my hand stung the seat of her pants and her look of betrayal caught my eye. She already was old enough to perceive the difference between a deserved spanking and this angered blow that was more a release of my frustration than an effort to discipline in love. That night as we prayed together I asked for the forgiveness of God and the forgiveness of that three-year-old. I promised her that though I knew I needed to discipline her when she deserved it, by God's grace I would never hit her again in anger.

If she had had no higher authority in life than me, she would have been crushed to despair by my shortcomings, and I would have tended to wear some false mask of ego to try to hide the fact that her hero was imperfect. Fortunately, she now understands that God, her truly highest authority, is in every way perfect and is my Lord and Savior just as he is hers. In that shared understanding, we can pursue those precious moments of reconciliation whenever we need to.

The second payoff of memorizing Scripture at home is apparent when dealing with crises. If one of the kids is selfishly hoarding a toy, I could skip the lecture and instead say, "Brady, what's the verse from Philippians we learned last night?"

"Have this attitude in yourselves which is also in Christ Jesus."

"Great job, Buddy. What kind of attitude did Jesus have, anyway?"

"A good one," he answers soberly.

"Was it selfish or unselfish?"

"Unselfish."

"Okay, what kind of attitude are you wrestling with right now?"

"Selfish." (He said it. I didn't have to.)

"Is that what you want to have today?"

"No, sir."

"What would Jesus do, Brady?"

"Change his attitude and give Cooper the toy."

"Will you do that?"

"Yes, sir."

It worked for us time after time after time. It's amazing how God's Word fits every situation. Just as he promises, "My word . . . will not return to me void."

God's Word is eternal. It transcends time, and that means it also fits with custom-tailored accuracy the life of each child, regardless of age. From preschool to high school graduation and beyond, God's Word always contains the building blocks for true maturity.

Working just a little every day, I find it easy to help even small children memorize Scripture. In our family, we began with each child at age three, and we continued practicing with them until they went off to college.

As the teen years approached in our home, we began another daily pattern that was really a Grand Slam. (If I could start over again, I would begin it much sooner.) First thing in the morning, we all piled into one bed and had a short family devotional, focusing on applying the principles from the verse we memorized the night before. The most interesting "family devos" were the ones led by one of the kids after a fifteen-minute shared planning time with me the day before.

Honestly, it was the very best thing in our day!

For Teens Too

Whenever I take a trip with a group of teenagers, we plan not only a lot of crazy, fun experiences but also a Scripture memory project—a short chapter that we learn along the way, reviewing it each time we make a stop. When the trip is complete, we return home with much more than exciting memories and empty pockets—we've also invested into our hearts a portion of God's eternal, protective Word.

discipline \di-se-plen\ n. 1. Security in action. 2. "This hurts me more than it hurts you." 3. Payment for a misdeed, "called" in fairness. 4. Because love cares enough to rend the very best.

18

Discipline Is a Lifestyle

The rod and reproof give wisdom.
—PROVERBS 29:15

So parents take heed, for your child is in need
of this balance of firmness and love.

"If you scream one more time, I'll give you a tranquilizer," the young mother threatened.

Even the takeoff roar of the 747 jet engines couldn't muffle the piercing, continuous screams of her three-year-old daughter in the seat just behind mine. Everyone on board was wishing these two had stayed at home.

The child was begging for discipline. She knew instinctively that her bottom needed firm attention. But her mother didn't have the loving courage to give it, or perhaps she was addicted to yet another new and illusory theory of child development. Her ultramodern remedy for the undisciplined child was medication. In twelve or fifteen years, another drug addict will roam the streets looking for an instant fix.

"Discipline me!" "Give me rules!" "Punish me when I break them!" By our very nature, we cry out for discipline, and the Bible commands us to lovingly discipline our children. Discipline minus love equals rebellion, but love minus discipline equals insecurity.

We are a nation of extremes. Our tea must be either piping hot or Arctic-ice cold. Our famous football players are giants, and our heralded gymnasts are tiny tots. We don't simply eat right—we crash diet. We don't just jog—we run marathons. So it is with our disciplinary tactics. Many children I counsel are so beaten down physically or emotionally, they can't see straight. They think their middle name is Shut Up and their backside is their father's belt rack.

With girls from this background, the first guy who comes along and says "I love you" will usually find a gullible sex object. With the boys, if they can't get rid of their aggression on the football field, a six-pack of beer and a Saturday night street fight will almost always be enticing. Both sexes are easy prey for drug pushers, and neither has a fraction of a chance to maintain a happy marriage.

Or flip the coin and meet the Sugar Lump kids. Their mothers are really their attorneys, rushing quickly to their defense if anyone (including their passive fathers) tries to correct or scold these little princes and angels. The fathers are usually not around enough to see the impending problem or to know their children's true needs.

And so, at an early age these kids squeal, grunt, and stomp when they're unhappy or don't get their way, and bang their trays when they're hungry. The girls at age six have the latest hairstyle and designer clothes, are wearing makeup a few years later, and by the time they enter junior high look as much like sixteen-year-old models as their genetics will allow.

For both boys and girls, any problems at school are always the teacher's fault. In their sports the coach is never right and the referee always needs new glasses.

Their early employment years are marked with failures and firings, and their marriages by selfishness and separation. When crises come in their lives, they fall apart, inside and out.

> Protesting a midnight curfew, a seventeen-year-old in Los Angeles calls his mom a four-letter name and slams the door in a rage, leaving his dad speechless and withdrawn.

In Chicago, a fifteen-year-old dreams up new ways to hurt her mom in daily acts of rebellion, because her mom stands in the way of her relationship with a boyfriend who time after time has demonstrated deceitfulness and immaturity.

"You're too old fashioned!" screams the Kansas City seventeen-year-old boy. "You never let me do anything, so I'm going on my own now." His single mother is tired of fighting. All she ever wanted for her son was his happiness, but he's ended up a spoiled, hot-headed misfit.

Andy reports to summer camp with deep bruises across his upper legs and an aggressive, unpredictable personality. Day after day he tests his counselor. He never adjusts to his cabin mates and seems to believe that anything he wants badly enough, he can get with his fists and elbows.

Marks of a Lifestyle

True discipline is a lifestyle. Making it happen depends on our following some basic rules. These ten guidelines are simple enough to write out, but living them out requires constant, relentless attention.

1. The sooner in the child's life you begin, the easier it is.
2. Mom and Dad can discuss their separate philosophies on discipline behind closed doors, but when they enter the arena, they should be of one mind—always supporting each other in discipline decisions.
3. If the rod is spared the child is spoiled, but if the rod is used in the wrong place or with the wrong motives or the wrong timing, the child will rebel at it every time.
4. Be careful about threats. If you warn a child to expect a certain kind of punishment, always follow through completely.
5. When a child breaks a rule, something corrective always needs to happen. For example: Lying always receives a spanking.
6. If respect is demanded in every conversation at home, heavy discipline will be required less frequently.

7. Every corrective action should be encircled by ten expressions of positive encouragement.

8. Spankings should always be both preceded and followed by expressions of love and support.

9. A child must be taught to cry softly and never be allowed to scream in rebellion.

10. Never give up on a child

These guidelines transcend personality differences and work with every kind of child—as we've learned in raising a stoic one, a jubilant one, a strong-willed one, and a compliant one.

Laying the Foundation: The Words and Ways of Discipline

One of the first words our children learned to say was *please*. For the first few months, it came out only as a *puh* sound, but even then nothing was given until that sound came out. Squeals, grunts, and banging a plate got no rewards.

Another early word was *ta-ta* (one-year-old lingo for *thank you*). After it was learned, if it wasn't said, the reward was taken back.

It's amazing how easy it was to develop an attitude of gratefulness in a child with these simple ground rules. The child learned early that the world did not revolve around his or her needs and wants.

Understanding the meaning of a soft but firm *no* was also part of our children's early training. We left plants, antiques, and lamps where they looked best in the house, and as soon as a one-year-old reached for one of them, that child heard *no* and had something else placed in his or her hands that was okay to play with. The second time the child reached for the forbidden item, he or she received a similar warning. The third time, the hand was slapped. We then encouraged the child and gave a hug to assure him or her of our love.

Depending on the child's strength of will, that particular plant or lamp might become a battleground for several confrontations. But by being consistent, firm, and loving, we ensured that the lesson was never forgotten.

Yes, sir, and *yes, ma'am,* also were early vocabulary. *Yeah* was not acceptable. We believed respect for parental authority was something to be forged continuously. A good husband never lets his wife be spoken to disrespectfully, and vice versa. In a two-parent home, respect is best learned by the child as parents model it toward each other. Likewise, the most effective way to teach sacrificial love is for mom and dad to put each other first. The example of my mom and dad in this has been easy to follow, because they have always modeled a mutually submissive relationship.

More important, the reinforcing steel in the foundation of respect is a healthy fear of God and his commandments. A disciplinary system built on that foundation will require few spankings—but physical punishment will still on occasion be required.

My dad clearly laid down the basics in our family: "When you break a rule, you're going to be punished." He never hit us anywhere but on the bottom. He never left bruises, but he always left an impression.

The last whipping he gave me was one I'll never forget. I was a cocky junior high kid, and I got caught lying to my mom. It was a Friday night. All my daddy said was, "Bring me my belt on Sunday afternoon."

He said nothing more to me about it the rest of that evening or all day Saturday, but the discipline was taking its full effect. I lived that lie a hundred times before he met me on Sunday afternoon. The spanking was the easy part for me, because during the interim, Daddy had accomplished two things. First, he allowed himself to calm down. I think he knew he would have hurt me if he spanked me in his anger immediately following my rebellious lie. Second, he let me discipline myself for a day and a half.

After the spanking, Mom was there to help Daddy reassure me that even though I had broken one of the cardinal rules of the house, I was still dearly loved.

Daddy was a good disciplinarian because he was fair and because he was firm. My first speeding ticket cost me my driver's license for a month. Daddy made it clear that the second would cause it to disappear for six months, and the third one would bring a year of no driving, no matter what came up during the penalty time. I knew that evacuating town for a tornado wouldn't have been enough reason for me to drive until the discipline was complete. I didn't get that second ticket until after I left home.

If I or one of my brothers got spanked at school, instead of criticizing the principal or coach or finding fault with the system, Daddy would spank us again when we got home.

He could discipline us for any kind of drinking, smoking, cheating, or use of bad language because he never did any of those. And watching him stay under the speed limit while driving over the years has helped make it seem right to obey the law.

He wasn't perfect—and he was well aware of his weaknesses—but he was totally sold on being an example to his kids. We were three hard-headed boys with all the normal adolescent energies, and each of us has made some very stupid mistakes in our lives, but the strong foundation of discipline my parents relentlessly built has always gotten us through. They made it easy to come back to the roots of serving, loving, and respecting one another in the family.

Tough Love

When I met Wesley at a monthly skating-rink youth rally, he was fourteen and had just been suspended from school for ten days.

Ten years later I paid for his attorney to get him a second trial after he spent six long years in a state penitentiary for armed robbery. In the years between, Wes had been caught breaking the law eighteen times.

Wes's dad was an alcoholic and wasn't at home to discipline him. His mom didn't know how. And the juvenile officer just kept putting off his punishment.

When his time was finally paid and his young adulthood was behind him, he was released. He was convinced he was a new person. But he had been ingrained with the philosophy that not much really happens when you do something wrong. He had only been disciplined once, so he continued smoking grass, drinking, and committing crimes.

One night he was caught with a firearm—shooting a warning shot in a fight—and authorities found a marijuana joint in his pocket. He called me (his only friend), and I went to see him. I found him lonely, frightened, clinging to the bars, and pleading for me to "put up the bond and get me out of this horrible place."

But I had made one of the toughest decisions I've ever had to make. "No, Wes, I'm not going to get you out this time. You've repeatedly ripped people off since you've been out of prison, and now it's time to pay. I want you to be free, but I want more for you to build your character.

You've got to grow up, Wes, and realize that when you do something wrong you must pay for it, all of it."

Not long afterward he called me from jail. While we talked of his upcoming trial, an operator came on the line with an emergency call. I quickly said goodbye to Wes, then took the call. It was a neighbor telling me he had just seen two boys steal a new eight-horsepower gasoline motor from our lakefront. We used it for a boat pump. To them it would make a nice go-cart engine.

I jumped into a boat to pursue the suspects. After a chase, I caught them. By this time the father of one of the boys had allowed them to hide the stolen motor in his trailer. But the boys—scared of the police, scared of me, and scared of jail—confessed.

"Will you press charges?" they asked.

Having learned my lesson with Wes, I looked intently into the faces of those two confused teenagers and replied, "I'm not concerned about the pump, but I'm deeply concerned about you. Yes, I'm going to press charges, and I hope they lock you up for a while." (I knew they wouldn't, but I wanted that impression to last as long as possible.)

mother \muth-er\ n. 1. The person in your home who is an expert at everything. 2. The biggest influence on a child's life.

19

My First Lady

How do I love thee? Let me count the ways.
—Elizabeth Barrett Browning

It was the night before I would walk out onto the gridiron for my first day of college coaching. I went into my bedroom, and there my wife of fourteen months calmly informed me that the flame in her heart for me had gone out and another had been lit for my best friend. The next day, she moved home, and not long afterward my best friend informed me of their wedding plans.

I cried every day for three months.

For some reason, forgiveness has never been a problem—she is a terrific lady and he's a wonderful man, and I never blamed either of them for the departure. Yet the hurt planted a deep scar on my heart that I'll die with.

Divorce is not only biblically wrong but also a devastating experience for the one who is left, as well as, eventually, for the one who leaves. And when children are involved—as my extensive teen counseling has proven to me repeatedly—they're especially broken by it, and their own hurts are seldom really considered or even understood.

But today I have a mysterious perspective about what that marriage failure meant in my own experience: I believe it was the greatest thing that ever happened to me. In the same way that God turned the pain, the rejection, and the ugly death of his Son into his most victorious moment in history, God also used my divorce to teach me how to love.

The only person alive who fully appreciates sight is someone who has been blind but has undergone surgery and received sight.

I was blind,and needed surgery, and God allowed it.

Losing a love taught me how to find one.

Later, when Debbie-Jo said "I will," and then twelve months later said "I do," I was like the ugly toad who had just been kissed by the lovely princess. I'll never forget our seventh date when I first kissed her: I melted. Last night, I kissed her again for perhaps the ten-thousandth time. It was so much like the first, yet so much more wonderful.

Romans 8:28 is indeed a reality: "And we know that God causes all things to work together for good to those who love God, to those who are called according to His purpose."

We know.

All things.

For our good.

God is able—infinitely able—to make it happen, just as his Word claims.

A dear old friend of mine suffered for years through the agonizingly slow decline and eventual death of his diseased wife. After a few years, he remarried. His new wife was healthy and able to give him her love and affection. I remember watching her brush his gray hair as if he were her childhood dream come true.

Big, tender tears flowed from his eyes. No one had ever done that for him before.

I know how he felt. Oh, to be appreciated! Our hearts hunger for the taste of it.

Debbie-Jo, my First Lady, does that for me. Whenever she wears a new wrinkle or a gray hair first appears, I count it as a sign of her ever-deepening love for me.

I remember hiding her engagement ring as the surprise in a box of Cracker Jacks, buried deep in the caramel corn and peanuts. I carefully resealed the box wrapper to keep it from looking tampered with. I pictured the look of surprise she would have.

We drove to the top of a three-hundred-foot cliff overlooking a vast Ozark lake . . . a Kodak perfect setting. The moment was rare. She opened the Cracker Jacks, took a bite, then sputtered. It tasted like the rubber cement I had used to reseal the package. She tossed the box over the cliff.

I caught it just as it left her hand. "Wait!" I screamed. "What about the surprise? It won't be stale!"

She squealed with excitement when my dear Grandmother's diamond caught her eye.

I was so much in love that day, though, really, I was just beginning to know what love was about. Nearly twenty-five years later, I feel I'm still discovering how to love her.

I don't recommend that anyone else try the same formula I did. But somehow God takes the broken pieces and puts them together in a new and more beautiful picture.

Why does it often take a tragedy to learn the lesson? Perhaps you will not wait to make the discovery until your children are gone from home or you receive your first social security check. Perhaps it won't require a two-by-four across the skull to open your eyes, as it did for me.

A Success Story

Darrell and Norma were first-class newlyweds. With Federal Express speed, Darrell would come home from his medical practice each day to spend precious moments with his new bride.

Soon, daughter Tracy was born, then came Michael and finally Jason. The young mom and dad defied all the odds against raising polite, courteous, moral children. Their enthusiasm for those three trophies beat any I've ever observed in a family. A twenty-by-twenty family room in their home is literally wallpapered with a thousand or more pictures that highlight every experience of those three children's growing-up years. I honestly get more energy standing in that room than I did in my first visit to the executive wing of the White House.

But, as the three children grew up and their parents spent their entire mental and emotional resources on their kids, Darrell and Norma grew apart from each other. They began to live like strangers in their home. A cloud of bitterness veiled the two hearts that once thrilled each other in romance. A separation loomed in the foreseeable future.

But many of us who knew them prayed . . . and we prayed . . . and we prayed.

The countdown to their last child's high school graduation grew ever closer to zero. Divorce seemed inevitable.

Then God moved.

Darrell's medical practice took a jolt: Two hard-to-replace employees had to leave, a long-time partner also left, and Darrell had to move his office to a new location. Just as he neared the autumn of his life, the season when he needed to begin slowing down, the pressure intensified.

He was drowning, reaching out for a rescue buoy. In desperation, he turned to his wife . . . and Norma responded.

All the creative energies with which she had so successfully planned holidays and birthday parties and teen dances for her children were now channeled toward her husband's world. She filled the two vacated support jobs in his practice while also directing the completion of the new office—a six-month project. News of her expertise spread through the medical community, and literally hundreds of doctors and nurses came by the new office to behold the results of her talented resourcefulness.

Unaware of what was happening, I called Darrell and Norma's home for what I expected to be yet another counseling and consoling conversation about misery revealed. Norma answered and told me the story—and literally made me stand up in the airport phone booth with excitement. I asked her twice if I had dialed the wrong number.

Here was a brand-new First Lady full of love and an enriched self-image fostered by her husband.

"Do you know how to hug and kiss your new lover?" I asked.

"I'm a quick learner," she quickly replied.

The next time I flew into town, I visited their house to behold this eighth wonder of the world. I spent the first half hour with Darrell, who praised Norma and the God who made possible the renewal of his marriage. When Norma joined us, she spoke of Darrell as if he were her Prince Charming. Later, I was given a tour of the new office, which Norma showed off in dignity and joy as the place where she loved to serve her husband.

teenager\teen-ag-er\ n. 1. A lifetime of possibilities wrapped up in hormones and acne.

20

The Teenage Years
... the Best Years

When a child turns thirteen, you put him in a
barrel with only a hole to feed him through.
When he turns eighteen, plug the hole.
—MARK TWAIN

I relate well to the continuing arms reduction discussions between the world's superpowers. As our children grew into their adolescent years, the missiles seemed to fly through our house with increased regularity.

One that was well targeted came from my oldest daughter one day in her twelfth year. Jamie's eyes—big and brown like her mother's—had that look of warning in them that I've grown to treat with highest caution. Over the years I've often seen the same expression on her mom's face, and it always meant, "You better listen, honey."

"Dad," Jamie said, "guess what's going to happen to you in a few months."

Mentally groping to figure out the bombshell (I hoped the IRS didn't have a problem with my latest tax return), I responded calmly, "What, sweetheart? I don't have a clue."

Her "Beware!" look didn't change. "I'm going to turn thirteen, and you're going to have a teenager on your hands."

The way she said it, I would have thought our house was about to be burglarized. I didn't know whether to panic, to board up the windows, or to borrow my brother's handcuffs and straitjacket (from his days as a policeman), and lock her up.

"A teenager, huh? Sounds like fun." It sounded crazy.

Having launched her missile—intermediate range, multiple warhead—she walked away.

The teenage years. It's a time when kids go through so many changes—and so do their aging parents. It's a time when communicating the all-important "I believe in you" in words they understand is a challenge indeed—since *teenspeak* is an altogether different language, and by the time you finally master it, it changes.

But thanks to having spent much time in a laboratory with other people's teenagers—as well as having many in-depth conversations with close friends who are effectively parenting teenagers—I'd discovered a few kernels of wisdom we relied on to help us make that stage in our kids' growth a satisfying adventure for all of us.

Here's a condensed list of those principles. I offer them in the hope that they help you bring out the best during your children's teen years.

Every parent is naturally stronger in some of these areas than in others, and we tend to emphasize too much what we're good at. If we're merciful, we tend to be a pushover and let the kids run the house. If we're well disciplined, we tend to beat our kids to death with rules and reminders. The word *balance* needs to be plated with 24-karat gold and hung over the bathroom mirror for every mom and dad to read each morning.

1. Callused Knees

As my children became teenagers, I realized all over again how the job of parenting was a lot bigger than my abilities. That meant a lot of prayer.

The Lord says, "You have not because you ask not," and "Ask, and you will receive, that your joy may be full." I figure that if one prayer is good, a thousand would be great. In this critical matter of raising teenagers, I wanted to get as close as possible to achieving Paul's directive to "pray without ceasing."

We could expect to have our children at home for only six teenage years. So during those years, I concentrated in prayer for them, asking God to make those years six golden years. I prayed for godly hearts. I prayed for their sexual purity. I prayed for their ability to stand alone. And I prayed for their spouses. The youngest of our four is now sixteen years old.

We ask with faith. God can do it. As Romans 8:32 suggests, if God thought enough of us to give us his Son, won't he also give us all things—including the wisdom and strength and love to help her make the most of this season in her life?

So, we prayed. We prayed for all the people in their lives: their friends, their teammates, their teachers and coaches, their future mates. We prayed for their ability to withstand peer pressure. We prayed for their self-images. We prayed for their desire to honor and obey us. We prayed for our wisdom in guiding them. And I prayed that the example of my life would be more consistently godly.

2. Elephant Ears

The teen years demand a parent who's eager to listen, slow to speak, and full of understanding. Every teenager is different, and getting to know each one well means a lot of listening and learning.

One of our daughters talked about everything (and I mean everything). The other was much quieter. We tried to be prepared constantly to enter an open door into her heart whenever she was in the mood to share her thoughts and feelings. Those opportunities came at the most unexpected times and often involved hurt or crisis. When those moments came, I wanted to be ready.

3. Heart to Heart

In these crazy years, my relationship with my children was everything. When trendy music and the media were telling them the way to have fun was through sex, drugs, and alcohol, and when peers were telling them that their parents were no longer relevant, I wanted to be the person they loved being with the most.

When I ran errands, I'd invite a teenager to come along. When their sports teams had a game, I wanted to be there. If I was speaking at a youth rally, there was a place for them on "the team" that put it on. When my girls came home from a party, their "late date" was with me. After my boys came home from a date a good "bowl of cereal" together made a great late night "How did it go?" debriefing session.

Several years ago, a good buddy of mine (and an excellent counselor of teens) was leading a parenting seminar at our camp during a twenty-four-hour Parents' Day at the end of their children's two-week camp session. He spoke about some of the principles in this book, and a father's hand shot up in protest near the back of the room.

"Yes sir, do you have a question?" my friend asked.

The man stood up, clearing his throat with deliberateness. "You may talk about all this theoretical hodge-podge," he said, "but when it comes to reality, that kind of thing just doesn't fly."

Other parents who were successfully applying these principles took the challenge off my friend's hands and told the man how they had seen them work in their own homes. The man quieted down, but at dinner after the seminar, he and his wife encountered my friend again with more rebuttal.

It just so happened that later that night the man's son was to compete in a camp swim meet. Also that night, the United States basketball team was playing in a televised game at the Olympics. As he and his wife were talking with my friend, the man looked at his watch and said suddenly, "Good grief, honey, we've got to get back to the motel. Tip-off time for the game is in fifteen minutes."

Of course the principles my friend spoke about were hodge-podge in that man's home.

Olympic basketball games may come only every four years, but when you need to spend time with your kids, there are always enough excuses and distractions around to keep you from it. No matter how eloquently we phrase our excused absences, adolescents especially have a built-in baloney detector. To them, our actions give a loud and clear signal: You're only priority number thirty-seven in my life.

4. Penetrating Eyes

The most important people for a teenager's parents to know are that teen's friends. The Bible declares that "bad company corrupts good morals." I've seen it happen a thousand times and need no convincing that it's as infallible as every other biblical truth. "When you lay down with dogs," the saying goes, "you get fleas."

So I wanted to know the character of my children's friends—to know them down to their very marrow. My children went out with good friends, or they didn't go. It was a ground rule. If they wanted to "hang out" with friends we didn't know yet, then they "hung out" at our house. We talked to them and tried to become their friends as well. We also made telephone calls and found out more about them.

The earlier you begin this with your kids, the more success you'll have with it.

5. Mannequin Body

Teenagers are notorious experts on their parents' weaknesses. That fact doesn't demand our perfection, but it does demand our giving strict attention to our habits, especially in the critical area of how we treat our bodies. For my children's sake—as well as for my wife's and myself—I cranked up the example on this one!

Be fully aware that the really "in" things for most teenagers are getting high on drugs and alcohol. If you pop pills (prescription or not), why can't they pop pills (prescription or not)? If you drink a beer to relax, why can't they have one—or even smoke a joint—to take the edge off their anxieties? If you haven't already discovered it the hard way, as have so many couples whom I've observed in the aftershock, the "legal" issue just doesn't fly with teenagers nowadays. They're too discerning—and too logical—not to see through it. A friend of mine recently confronted his fifteen-year-old daughter with the legal aspect of her drinking bouts, and she snapped back, "Why don't you drive fifty-five?"

The same logic applies in every aspect of our behavior. If we tell little lies (which may be larger than we admit), why can't they tell little lies (which may be larger than they admit)? If we rent R-rated videos, why can't they watch one at a theater? If we pay to see and hear performers talk and act immorally, what's so wrong with teenagers talking the same language and acting out the same scenes with their friends?

Kids measure our values by how we spend our time and how we spend our money—not by what we preach.

6. Steady Hand

A steady hand is one that's careful with handouts.

The extras in life that my children legitimately desired were not theirs simply for the asking. Privileges came with proven responsibility. Freedom always traveled with accountability. Payment was the reward for hard work. Giving was mutual. More giving followed the evidence of gratitude.

I owed my children beds.

I owed them adequate food.

I owed them educational opportunities.

I owed them a good home.

I owed them a sound example of godly living.

I owed them a biblical foundation for life.

But the accessories were privileges to be earned. Talking on the phone (which I pay for) is a privilege. Going out at night (and keeping me up) is a privilege. Spending five dollars (that I have earned) at McDonald's is a privilege.

If you feel your adolescent is beginning to kick against the restraining walls and needs to understand in more detail the freedom/responsibility balance, you may want to use the six-level system shown on the following pages, a system that many parents have adopted in various forms. The presentation here is only a suggested guideline. I strongly recommend that you draw up your own system of levels that meet with your particular standards.

The great thing about a system such as this is that teenagers can choose the level on which they decide to live—having whatever freedoms they choose to have but always with the corresponding responsibilities.

Levels of Freedoms and Responsibilities

Level 1

Living in a youth detention home—no freedom. The psychologists and authorities decide everything.

Level 2

Living at home, but with no freedom—no phone use, no money to spend, no nights out. We take you to school, and we pick you up after school. Weekends are spent at home.

Level 3

Freedoms

1. One five-minute phone call per night.
2. One night out per weekend, with an 11 P.M. curfew.
3. One television show (approved by us) per day.

Responsibilities

1. Obedience to parents.
2. Respect for parents evident at all times.
3. Chores done at home consistently.
4. Complete honesty with parents and teachers.
5. No use of alcohol, drugs, or tobacco.
6. Clean language at all times.
7. Social time limited to friends with good, stable reputations.
8. Let parents know specific plans—where you are and for how long—at all times.
9. No unexcused absences in school.
10. "Good deportment" slips signed weekly by teachers.
11. Grade average: _____.

Level 4

Added Freedoms

1. Up to thirty minutes on the phone per night.
2. Curfew on weekend night out extended till midnight.
3. One night out during the week until 11 P.M.
4. Monitored spending—set at ___ per week.
5. Driving to and from school.
6. On two afternoons per week: two hours free time after school.

Added Responsibilities

1. Always ready for school on time and for bed on time, without parental reminders.
2. Extra help provided regularly for Mom and Dad in housework, yardwork, etc.
3. Daily quiet time with God.

4. Regular attendance at church.
5. Regular attendance at church youth meetings.
6. Grade average: _____.

Level 5

Added Freedoms

Increased from Level 4 in accordance with your interests and desires and Mom and Dad's standards.

Added Responsibilities

Increased from level four in accordance with your own needs for character growth and Mom and Dad's standards.

Level 6

Living away from home and able to maintain a lifestyle reflecting high moral values.

child \child\ *n.* 1. Comes into the world with acute pain and intense joy. 2. One in whom you invest your very heart. 3. One you love with the intent of letting go.

21

Crossroads

What is your child like?
Who is he?
He is not as he sees himself.
He is not as you see him either.
Your child is as he sees himself in your eyes.

Time. Time. Waiting. Waiting.
Movement. Wonder.
Waiting. Waiting.
Waiting.
Pangs. Hospital. Nurses. Pangs. Fear. Pressure. Hurt. Breathing. Timing.
Time.
Waiting. Patience. Husband. Close. Sharing.
Pain. Pain!
Increased.
Pain!
Intense. *Pain!* Doctor!
Pain!
Push! *Pain.* Push!
Birth!

Life . . .

A child. Ours. Healthy. Beautiful.

Tears. Beginning. Dreams. Sharing. Happy. Telephone.

Ours. Likeness. Tiny. Mystery. Eyes—Mom's. Fingers—Dad's. Mouth—Grandma's. Nose—Grandpa's.

Rest. Plans. Dreams. Nursing. Rest. Dreams. Hopes. Talking. Laughing. Sharing. Tomorrow.

Home. Us.

Crying. Feeding. Diapers. Schedule. Crying. Feeding. Diapers. Night. Tired. Late. Early. Rash. Reality.

Tiny. Warm. Cuddling. Ours! Dreams. Future.

Days. Weeks. Months.

Every day. New. Recognition. Smiles. Sounds. Playful. Sitting. Crawling. Giggling. Close. Hugs. Tomorrow.

Step. Fall. Step. Steps. Good! Yes! Steps. Stumble. Steps. Yes! Success. Dreams. Plans.

Year. Years.

Talk. Play. Run. Sing. Make. Climb. Laugh. Grow.

Questions. Questions. Questions. God. Where? Heaven. Heart. Ask. Jesus. Loves. Me.

Begin. School. Teacher. Bus. New. Playground. Friends. Fun. Acceptance. Rejection. Hurt. Questions.

Home. Hugs. Talk. Bedside. Pray. Snug. Sleep.

> While. You. Quietly. Watching.
> Praying.
> Dreams.
>
> Morning.
> Love. Encourage. Discipline. Hug. Love.
> Live. Example. Pray.
> Meals. Hands. Held. Hearts. Warm.
> Scripture. Pray. Play. Work. Together.
> Talk. Listen.
> Show. Share. Shape.

Summers. Winters. Years.

TV. Funny. Flashy. Smart.
"Love." Sex. Drinks. Smiles. Laughs. Lies.
Tough. Faces. Hate. Blood. Crash. Kill
Buy. Buy. Buy. Buy. Happy. Happy.
Lies.
NO!

Taller. Stronger. Learning. Helping. Wondering.
Wrong. Right. Growing. Going. Strong.

You. Work. Climb. Push. Go.
House. Committees. Clubs. Go. Status. Climb. Mine.
Go. Go.
Stretched. Thin. Tight. Fatigue.
Questions. No. Together. No.
Spend. Time. With. No.

Not. Fair.
Why?
Why?
Get. Attention.

No!
Lose. Temper.
Harsh. Hurt.
No!

No . . .
Stop. Wrong.
Forgive. Me.
Let's . . .

Back. Up. Back. Together.
Back. Yard. Talk.
Listen. Listen. Laugh. Hug.
Change.
Mend.
I. Really. Love. You.

Vacation? Really? Away. Together. Us.
Great. Time. See. Do. Explore. Great.
Back. Home. Different. Great!
Back. To. School.

Taller. Stronger. Different. Body. Changing.
Questions. Parties. Peers. First. Date. Weekends.

Wild. Challenge. Just. Try. Everybody. Does.
Music. Movies. Cars. More. After. Impress. Just. Watch.
Wild. Go. Get. Be. Free. Cool. Why. Not?

Fun. Fun? Free. Free?
Me. Who? How? When? Where? Am. I. Need.
What? Who? She. He. They. Me. Who? Where?
Am. I. Need. What? Who? Need. Time. Time.

Out. Late. Come. Home. Still. Up? Time. Milk.
Cookies. Talk . . .

Listen. Listen. Love. Encourage. Listen.
Think. Listen.
Offer. Ideas. Listen. Goals. Listen. Plans. Listen.
I. Love. You. Are. So. Special.
Listen. Listen. Time. Time.
Good. Night. Lights. Out. Quietly.
Praying.
Praying.
Time. Time. Time. Together. Plans. Together.
Work. Together. Dreams. Together. Getting . . .

Ready.
Graduation!
Leaving. Home.
Ready.
Ready.
Gone.

A child.
Ours. Healthy. Beautiful.
Remember? Birth! Life . . . A child. Ours. Likeness.
Sharing. Dreams. Future.
Time. Time. Time.
Time.
Ready?
Gone.

PART V

Tomorrow's Family Album

"I'm glad you're home!"

discovery \dis-ku-ve-re\ n. 1. Realizing the value and potential imbedded in your children. 2. The ability to see your children's inner resources and the determination to harness their energy for good.

22

The Generation That Followed Discovery

Within every young soul is a great vision for life,
awaiting nurture from the parent
who continuously dreams expectantly.

We have it all!

We have within us a God-given desire for intimacy with our children plus an innate yearning to carve our initials on their hearts as a lasting legacy—lending our dreams and values for building the trustworthy foundation of future generations.

Most of us have a satisfactory paycheck in return for a work week that is generally significantly shorter than that of our forefathers. We have both time and money to enjoy recreation and an occasional vacation together as a family.

We have the Bible and the Holy Spirit of God for daily guidance.

And we have our country's most valuable resource: not oil or gold or other material riches, but a home built around the marriage relationship that God gave us as a glimpse into the mysterious union between Christ, himself, and the church. Home—the most powerful place in the world.

To help us make that place the best it can possibly be, the resources available through youth ministries and parents' support groups are more abundant now than in all the previous generations combined.

We have unparalleled possibilities for fulfillment. Our treasure is vast . . . but not necessarily permanent. We can waste and lose it—like the people of ancient Greece and Rome—or, as the people of God we were meant to be, we can channel these true riches into the lives of our children.

If we truly make the *discovery* of how valuable our kids are and how vast their potential that can be released if we love them totally, then the generation that follows *discovery* will be like no other this world has seen.

Our sons and daughters can have the privilege, more than any other generation in history, of living life with all the joy and discipline and love and satisfaction that we were created to enjoy. They can be like a forest of unprecedented majesty, full of lush, towering trees that teem with fruitful branches.

Is this just fruit pie in the sky?

I don't think so. I see so many fruit-bearing trees nearing maturity. As I travel I see healthy trees rising up everywhere. One weekend I met a high school junior who told me, "Joe, my goal is to make my school the first Christian public school in America." I didn't catch what he meant till he continued, "By the time I graduate, I want everyone in my school to know the Truth." What vision! And you can bet that boy has a mom or dad, or both, who stand behind him all the way.

The week before, at a youth rally in a different state, I met a high school senior whose influence resulted in thirteen new student-led Bible study groups—one on each high school campus in her city. I also know the supportive mom who launched that girl's dream.

In the same city, a student body president sent birthday cards—loaded with scriptural truth—to all 1,500 kids in his high school.

I talk with hundreds of kids every year who say to their parents "Please" and "Thank you" and "Yes sir" and "Yes ma'am, I'll be happy to"—not out of fear, but out of a healthy respect for authority.

These kids may not be a great majority. But there is a growing "Who's Who in Moral Values," kids who lock elbows and encourage each other to say *no* to drugs, alcohol, and sex.

And there can be more.

I've seen a runaway sixteen-year-old come home to his daddy's smile and open arms.

I've marveled as a strung-out father revamped his life and work schedule to spend more time at home during his children's growing-up years.

I've seen parent and child embrace after they've really discovered each other at a camp or during a church retreat or on the other side of a tragedy.

And I've felt a quickened heartbeat after seeing one of my own children suppress natural, self-centered desires and instead imitate Christ in a critical area of life.

I hope that you, too, have a glimpse of the unfathomable riches of these things that give life such a passion.

The resources, the riches, the momentum . . . we've got to believe it will work and harness all that energy.

The search for something better can help make it happen in the face of the sheer frustration of trying to find happiness and fulfillment through chemicals or sex outside marriage or fame or fortune, the nagging fear about AIDS, the rising disillusionment with the New Age, or the utter emptiness of passing fads.

Sure, outside pressures counterattack with relentless force.

But I believe that by far the great majority of children who are given at least one good adult friend who has made the *discovery* will choose to have their own personal walks with Jesus Christ and to pattern their lives after his.

And the generation that follows *discovery* will be a pleasure indeed to live in.

celebrate \se-le-brat\ v. 1. To jump for joy and leap with laughter. 2. To hang balloons and make ballyhoo; to have fun and play games. 3. To kiss and make up.

23

Dancing

The older I get, the luckier I am.
—BILL COSBY

I know it has only been through God's amazing grace that I can ever call myself a parent—especially one whose crown is adorned with four children I've been admiring almost heroically the more I get to know them.

One night as I tucked my fourteen-year-old Jamie into bed (I guess they'll never outgrow that as long as they live in this house), we spent our usual fifteen to twenty minutes together—praying, memorizing and reviewing Scripture, and discussing the day's events. But that night was unusually special. Jamie began to ask questions about her professional career, which loomed in the not-so-distant future. Later, something she prayed moved me to gratitude. "Dear Jesus," she said, "thank you for Mom and Dad who love me so much. I want to be just like them some-day."

I reflected for a few moments on our thousands of bedtime talks and the hunk of Scripture we'd committed to memory. I thought back on all our daddy-kid days . . . the countless gymnastics meets and volleyball games . . . the family trips far and wide . . . and the tearful hugs that followed some significant spankings. I thought of the "imbalance" of my life—weighted toward time with my kids and away from any hobbies and interests outside the home. I smiled . . . knowing I wouldn't trade any of these times for any presidential office or a six-figure paycheck.

I looked at my little prize snuggled in her feather pillow and said to her, "Peanut, thanks for saying that. But there's something you need to know. I've always looked up to you. You're one hundred times better than I ever dreamed of being. You'll do things in your lifetime I couldn't begin to do. And I've loved every minute of being your daddy."

There's a lot about heaven I don't know yet, but I do know enough to be sure I want to spend eternity there.

I'm also certain—and for this, dear God, I'll be forever grateful—that my four kids and their mom and one lucky dad are going to be there singing and dancing through those golden streets, laughing over the great family memories we've known in this house.

If you feel in your heart a new flicker of light and warmth for those you love most . . . then by all means fan the flame. Pour your creative energies into building up the blaze, and let it rage. Put your entire heart into your home, and watch the family scrapbook thicken with happy pages.

If you have a prodigal son or daughter, I pray you will know soon the euphoric rush of unimagined magnificence as that child returns to renew the closeness you once shared.

And if you have a spouse at home, I hope you'll make the soap operas blush as you pour yourself into that relationship.

Parenting wasn't designed as an experience to simply survive. We were meant to celebrate it . . . to succeed in it . . . to weep in both the hurts and the joys . . . and leave nothing behind to regret.

home \hom\ n. 1. A special place of refuge that harbors me and shuts out hurtful forces from the outside world. 2. Where pleasures meet you at the door—the smell of cookies baking . . . Mom's hug and Dad's smile . . . "I'm so glad you're home!" 3. Where no one yells at me. 4. Where hearts dwell truly in love. 5. What forever's for.

24

Discovery at Dawn

*A life is made up of a great number of small incidents and a
small number of great ones.*
—ROALD DAHL

Blessed are the pure in heart, for they shall see God.
—MATTHEW 5:8

I've seen a bride—or was it an angel?—adorned in pure white, radiant
as she made her once-in-a-lifetime journey down the aisle. When her
slender hands took mine and she pledged her lifelong troth to me, I felt
the way the first man to land on the moon must have felt. How beautiful
that day was . . . and how undeserving I was of such a prize!

And when that little bride gave birth to my first baby girl, I saw the
miracle of life. Air filled her lungs. Light invaded her squinting eyes.
And rushing through the countless miles of capillaries in her precious,
tiny body was blood carrying the mingled genetic codes of hundreds of
generations of brides and grooms.

I've seen God intertwining my heart with my daughter's in a response
as continuing as the ocean tides . . . then doing it once again with
another precious child, and another, and another.

I've been fortunate to witness tears of intense relief and happiness as teenage drug addicts and young prostitutes and prisoners find hope and life, all in a moment of renewal from God. It is indeed a miraculous sight to see a tiny seed slowly rupture and give way to rootlet and stem, later to become a sapling and, in time, a timber giant to cradle children in its branches. But to see a dead tree come back to life is so much the greater miracle.

I've watched the veil between time and eternity lift with wondrous ease as a fulfilled but fatigued old granddad tenderly closed his eyelids one last time in a moment of timeless peace.

Today at dawn came another discovery, as ten thousand shades of color were programmed into my eyes. In the minutes before sunrise, with a whisper of cirrus clouds lacing the eastern sky and cotton puffs of cumulus dancing nearby, morning's first rays sprayed their edges with a garden variety of reds and golds. Then, in a twinkling of an eye, a brilliant gold mine erupted. The fiery sun peeked over the mountain, inflaming the autumn hues of Ozark mountain foliage: from the orange and yellow of sassafras to the deep burgundy of black gum, with Indian-red sumac and multi-shaded maples and a hundred others.

I watched in amazement. Just for me, the Creator had painted a work of art unmatched in all the galleries of the world. I remembered the words of an old Galilean fisherman: "We were eyewitnesses of his majesty."

With that dazzling display lighting the way, my mind raced straight and sure to my most prized possessions: my bride, having become even more beautiful in the twenty-five fleeting years I've known her, the growing foursome who crown my life with significance by calling me daddy, my aging mom and dad who never grow weary of being my number one fans.

It was more than just another indescribable Ozark October sunrise. It was a rediscovery of the designer label that has trademarked my life since the time when there was no time . . . not the label of some Paris textile guru but of the Great Designer of a universe infinite and infinitesimal, where millions of galaxies are born at the blinking of His eye, and where the minds of Plato and Socrates are baffled by the metamorphosis of a helpless, ugly caterpillar into a butterfly dressed more beautifully than any queen who ever reigned.

I was personally designed, planned, and programmed to know this Creator . . . to know him with greater intimacy and completeness than I know my wife (who to this day puts butterflies into flight in my stomach whenever she holds my hand). I was designed for fulfillment—not any cheap, add-water-and-stir euphoria over a new title or promotion, a bigger paycheck, a sensual encounter, or an acquired jewel, but true, lasting fulfillment.

I, like you, am designed by God for the eternal.

And his plan was for me

> to receive it from a mom and dad,
>
> to participate in it with my bride, and
>
> (the most exciting adventure of all!)
>
> to pass it on to my children.

Just as the dawn's Designer gave me renewed perspective on my family life with this morning's sunrise . . . so I now pass this fulfilling focus on to you. It is appropriately mixed with tears and hugs and laughter and the holding of little hands around the dinner table, thanking Him for the experience.

promise \pro-mis\ n. 1. Commitments kept by the grace of God. 2. Being where you said you'd be, doing what you said you'd do. 3. Keeping them reaps eternal benefits.

25

Promise-Keeping Men Keep Promises to Their Children

God never made a promise that was too good to be true.
—Dwight L. Moody

As my son, Cooper, and I traveled to Pittsburgh, Pennsylvania, to address the Promise Keepers rally in Three Rivers Stadium, I knew I could only thank God for the grace he had given me to be a promise-keeping dad to my kids. So many failures had plagued my childhood and college years. Ultimate failure had ended my first marriage. Now, through an even more amazing grace, God had given me a second chance to "finish the race" and be a husband and a dad my family could count on. I could hardly keep from jumping off the platform that beautiful Saturday afternoon. I wanted so badly for the men in the stadium to "catch the grace" that God had given me. The principles I shared were the ones in this book. They work! All I can say is, they worked.

The years have fast-forwarded along since I first experienced the stories in this book. My oldest daughter called yesterday, so proud she was about to pop. "Daddy, you're going to be a gran'pa."

I didn't know what to say. I never thought I'd get to be a gran'pa. God introduced Jamie to her life love a few years ago, and they continue to love each other and love God like crazy. The bazillion prayers paid untold dividends. The countless breakfast table and bedside devotionals produced the fruit they promised . . . and then some. I can't boast about anything I've ever done right, but I made some radical promises to my wife and kids, and by God's grace, I was able to keep them. I promised to say "I'm sorry" when I blew it. (I can't count the times I had to ask for forgiveness!) I promised to be there when they needed me, no matter how many miles I had to travel to arrive on time. (Like landing a small plane in a cow pasture to get to a volleyball game!) I promised to be faithful to my bride. I promised to lie by my kids each night and memorize a Bible verse and pray. (Looking back, that was the finest of times!) I promised to open the Bible at the breakfast table and briefly tap into the wisdom God gave us there.

The payoff has been overwhelming. Last night, Cooper (now an adrenaline- and testosterone-infested sixteen-year-old) prayed, "Dear God, help me be a godly man." I jogged with my twenty-year-old Courtney early this morning, and she broke out in the middle of our jog in prayer and praise to the God she loves so very much. I came in after the jog and gave my silver-anniversary bride a back rub and spent a few minutes cherishing those tireless back and shoulder muscles that I've held in my arms so many wonderful nights and admired so many days as she labored through the storms of raising four from diapers to early adulthood.

My dream epitaph was spelled out for me last week when I encountered a gray-haired friend outside of our camp's chapel in the woods. I asked him how his week had been and his eyes filled with tears as he told me how tough it had been to bid a final farewell to his eighty-seven-year-old father-in-law, Allan Bjerre, for whom he had been providing in-home care for the past several years. My friend said that Allan had been married to his much adored wife, Lillian, for sixty-three years. Although Lillian was ninety-seven, divine providence would have it that she would outlive him. As my friend fed his dear father-in-law his last meal, his breathing became faint. The nurse entered the room and simply said to the beleaguered old fellow, "What is your name?"

Allan quietly whispered, "Allan."

The nurse then asked gently, "What is your wife's name?"

Allan paused and lovingly responded, "Lillian."

As her name passed softly through his lips, he breathed his last and fell into the arms of his Savior where his eternal reward would humbly be received.

This fall, I, too, said goodbye to a dear friend, Dr. Roberto Olivares, who passed through the curtain of the mortal to the immortal after a heroic thirteen-year battle with leukemia. As Dr. O. captured his last noble breaths, his wife and four kids caressed him, praised him, and soothed him in his pain with accolades too many to count. He ever so faintly bragged on his kids, expressing how wonderful each had been to him. He repeated two phrases in his final moments.

"God is good. God is so good. God is so good."

And then, peeking sheepishly from under his fatigued eyelids, he said to his wife, "I love her. I love her. I love her."

You know what? The gains and losses on NASDAQ didn't really matter that day. Wall Street couldn't have been further from his mind. His wife, his kids, and God were all that mattered . . . promises made . . . promises kept . . . promises to now unfold for eternity.

Joe White is author of eleven books—including *Pure Excitement*, which won the gold Medallion Teen Book of the Year for 1996, *Looking for Love in All the Wrong Places*, and *The Gift of Self-Esteem*—Joe White is a noted speaker on family and teen issues. He is the president of Kanakuk-Kanakomo Kamps, Inc., which hosts 14,000 campers each summer. He has spoken for such noted events as James Dobson's Focus on the Family, Promise Keepers, and Life on the Edge parent and teen conferences. White has four children, and has been married to his wife, Debbie-Jo for over thirty years.

Printed in the United States
85459LV00007B/100-102/A

9 781582 293417